Jake Does America: 10,000 Mile Trek

Jake Sansing

###

CONTENTS

###

###

###

1

I was fresh out of the Army and life was going pretty good. I had used most of the money I had made during my service to open an audio recording, mixing, and mastering studio in Humboldt, Tennessee. It wasn't the best place for business but I was making a decent profit.

After about a year of working as an engineer, one of my ex-girlfriends decided to snake her way back into my life. She talked me into selling everything in my studio so we could get a house together. I can put anything aside for someone if I love them. Just the kind of guy I am. Of course, that did backfire.

She ends up leaving me after just two months. I had sunk all my money into our new house. My studio was gone. There was no way to rent another building and furnish it with all the equipment I would need. I wouldn't be able to pay the upcoming rent on this house. So, I sell everything I have and now I'm homeless. At least I kept my car, though, so I can still manage to get a job.

I needed somewhere to think and be able to come up with some plans on what to do next. I ended up moving in with my parents. I didn't plan on staying long. Just long enough to find a job and start over. Everything had been swept out from under my feet so fast that I didn't know what to do. I'd get it all figured out, though.

One spring night, back in 2013, I was sitting in my room, when out of nowhere I go flying through the wall in front of me. One second I'm playing guitar and the next my head is underneath the bathroom sink. What in the world? A tornado had just thrown a tree through my parents' house and almost squashed me like a bug!

I was stunned. I never heard the wind picking up or anything. It was like a freak storm. My parents were still sleeping on the other side of the house and had no idea. I woke them up to tell them a tornado had just came through and there's a tree in the house. As I was walking back from their room I noticed a large branch sticking through the ceiling in both the kitchen and living room. Man, this is just great.

I walked outside to check out the damage and realized that my car had been smashed. My parents ran out and took shelter at my aunt's house, which was just next door, but I continued standing there in the rain; staring at this mangled up piece of metal that used to be my car. That was the only thing that I had left from the money I had made in the service. What a blow that was.

I only had liability insurance so I was screwed. A brand new Nissan Altima was now just a pile of junk. My chances of getting a job are now slim to none because we're in the middle of nowhere Greenfield, Tennessee. Whatever gleam of hope that was left inside of me vanished. It was like I didn't even care anymore.

I stuck around for a few days to help clean up all the damage left behind and put my car up for sale for $200. It still had a good engine in it but it was beyond repair. You would never be able to drive this thing legally. I was surprised that someone actually bought it. I'm assuming they just wanted to use or sell the parts from it. I could have made a little more money off it if I had done that but I just didn't care.

It ended up taking us about a month to repair all the damages around the house. If I wasn't working on the house then I was just lying on my bedroom floor, thinking about what I was going to do next. I felt like a zombie. I didn't want to live the rest of my life like this. I had to come up with something.

That's when I decided to walk across America. It may not fix anything but it definitely wouldn't hurt anything either. It was something that I had always wanted to do and there was nothing holding me back. I had never known exactly why I wanted to do a cross country hike but I figured this would be as good a time as any. I had about $700 to my name and that would be enough for the gear I would need.

I went to the library so I could get on a computer and purchase some hiking equipment. Before I made any purchases, though, I let some friends know what had happened and what I was about to set out to do. I was going to walk from Delaware to California. Everyone thought I was crazy and that I just needed to stay where I was and get my life back together. I saw this as a great opportunity, though, so I was taking it.

That's when this guy named Mike, who happened to live in Maryland, heard about what I was getting ready to do. He sent me an email explaining how he was planning to ride a bike across America, and that I was welcome to join him if I wanted. I tried convincing him to walk with me but he wasn't having that. I finally gave in and decided that I would cycle the country with them. It wasn't what I had always wanted to do but it was close enough and I'm sure I would enjoy the company.

After talking with Mike for a few days, making sure he was as serious about it as I was, I went ahead and purchased a bike along with saddle bags, a tent, sleeping bag, and you know, just the basic stuff that I would need. Then, to top it off, I bought a train ticket from Memphis, Tennessee to Washington, D.C.

After I had bought my gear and ticket I had about $200 left. That doesn't seem like much but money wasn't an issue at this point. If I could get going I was confident that I could make it work. If it came down to some sort of equipment failure that I couldn't afford to fix then I would just walk. No problem.

My gear finally comes a few days later and I immediately put it all together. I got to test ride my bike for a few days before it was time to leave. They say that you need to put at least a hundred miles on a bike before getting ready to tour on it. Seemed like it would be good enough to get the job done. Now, I needed to be in Memphis by August 20th to catch my train. That was about a one hundred twenty-mile bike ride from where I was at. I've never done any long distant cycling so I gave myself three days to make it on time.

August 16th finally rolls around and I've said my goodbyes to everyone. They were all still trying to talk me out of it. I'm not sure why they even bothered with that. Anyone that knows me knows that if I set my mind to something I'm going to do it. Tomorrow I would be out of there. Simple as that.

Out of everything I had been through in my life this was the last thing anyone needed to be worried about. This was a time for me to find myself, gather my thoughts, and just kind of reconnect with who I am. I was happy with my decision and I knew they would all see it eventually. It's hard to see the strength in someone when they're depressed, battling their own battles; but I thought I knew what I was doing.

It was time to start making my way for Memphis. The morning was nice and cool but I could tell that it was going to be a long and sweltering day. As the day progressed it became more and more difficult to make it from one small town to the next. It wasn't physically hard but I was sweating my water out just as fast as I could drink it.

At least fall and winter were well on the way. That much I did know and I had it planned that way. I didn't know what routes we would be taking. I just knew that I didn't want to be going through the desert once summer came back around and I figured Mike had the same idea.

As hot as it was, I had made it half way to Memphis by the end of my first day. I was really surprised given the circumstance. A hundred miles in 110°F left me feeling exhausted, but confident. Tomorrow I could ease up a bit. There was no rush to get into Memphis any earlier than I needed to. My only business there was to catch my train.

My first night out I camped behind a church. I spotted it off the highway just as it was getting dark. I got little sleep, though. It was just too hot and there was a storm making its way through. At least the storm got rid of all the pesky mosquitoes.

I'll admit that I did feel a bit miserable for my first day but not to the point of regret. Discomforts were to be expected. It wasn't anywhere near as bad as my army days, though. I knew I could get through this.

I tried to make the trip to Memphis last but I made it a day early. Memphis just isn't the place I'd like to be without a safe place to spend the night. I'd rather take my chances out in the wild than in a big city. However, since I was early, I made my way to a motel. I hated to do this because it felt like a waste of money but I was right down the road from the train station, and I knew I'd make it there on time.

The next morning, I packed up and made my way to the station. My train wasn't scheduled to leave until midnight so I sat at the station all day. There was an older man who sat beside me to keep me, or most likely himself, company. From what I gathered, that's just where he went for conversation. A good place for it I suppose; conversation and naps. No sleep for me, though. I was wide awake from the excitement of my upcoming journey.

The train finally arrived! It felt like it took forever but

once it came I wondered where all that time had gone. I guess I can thank the old man for that. I went outside to board up and head out. I climbed in, took my seat, and settled in for a long ride. My adrenaline had depleted and I was finally feeling drained. As we started down the tracks, leaving the lights and sounds of Memphis, the darkness approaching draped over me like a blanket. I fell fast asleep.

I had to switch trains in Chicago, Illinois where I would take my final ride into Washington, D.C. We were about an hour from Chicago when I woke up. Perfect timing to go downstairs into the kitchen area and grab a cup of coffee. The coffee was black, burned, and overpriced; but I didn't mind. The young man who sat with me didn't seem to mind either, although we did joke about it. We talked for the remainder of our ride into Chicago.

He was coming up to visit some family and I was getting ready to trek across the country. I hated the feeling of my conversation becoming the highlight but I suppose it isn't every day you hear someone mention something like that. He asked for my number so we could stay in contact. He wanted to keep up with how my journey was going and for me to send him pictures of the things I'd see along the way.

That's when I had the idea to create a blog on the Internet. I felt like I would probably run into a lot of people who were just as curious as he was. It would be a lot easier for people to follow a blog than to give each of them my phone number. I thought "Jake and Mike Do America" would be a good name for our adventure. I went ahead and set up our new site and would fill Mike in on it later.

A few hours had passed and I was on my last train to D.C. It was daylight this time, at least for a few more hours, and it was nice to see the countryside passing me by. I knew I'd be coming back through here so I tried not to pay too much attention. I didn't want to be spoiled by seeing something I'd see later on. I wanted everything to be new to me. Not knowing what to expect was part of the beauty of it.

I fell asleep and after another good night's sleep on the train I woke early in the morning as we were making our way through the Appalachian Mountains. I'd never been through the Appalachians before. It was quite the site with the fog still lingering in the valleys. I had the urge to get out at the next stop, which was a small town hidden deep in the mountains. The town looked like something out of a Tim Burton movie. I'd have to restrain myself, though. I had more coming my way than I could yet imagine.

It was probably about 2:00 p.m. when we pulled into the D.C. station. That gave me enough time to put my bike together and get out of there before it got dark. This was another one of those cities I didn't want to get stuck in. As a matter of fact, looking back at it, I always tried to camp before or after any towns that had a population greater than 2,000 people. I've always felt that when you get too many people together they get a little to frenzied for my liking.

As I was making my way towards California, MD, I passed by a few of the monuments in D.C. It was entertaining to see them in person instead of books. The Potomac River was an even better site for my eyes. I've always been drawn to water and mountains. I wanted to go down for a swim but I had to be on my way. I eventually made my way into the Cedarville State Forest. It was still hot but nothing like Tennessee. I'd get a good night's sleep here and be at Mike's house by tomorrow afternoon.

When I pulled up to Mike's house he was putting things away from a yard sale. I assumed that he was trying to gather up a few extra bucks for the trip as I had done before I left. I helped him put everything away and found my place to sleep for the night. There was a hammock hanging up in his front yard. That'd be my spot for the next week and then we would be on our way. Until then, we needed to get some plans together.

We decided that we would start our trek from Crisfield, MD but that was on the other side of the Chesapeake Bay. Luckily, he had a friend, Brady, who had a boat and was willing to give us a lift. We loaded up in his Brady's truck on September 1st and headed down for the boat ramp at Point Lookout State Park.

The water here looked calm but once we made it out of the boating area I was shocked to see how choppy the bay was. I was beginning to feel some concern now since the boat was barely large enough for the three of us. With the constant roll of those five-foot waves I could tell this was going to be a difficult cross.

We had made it about half way across the bay when we came up to an old lighthouse. I had our captain pull up next to it so I could climb up. The lower portion of the ladder had been eaten away by the salty sea water but, if I timed it right, I could let a wave lift me high enough to reach one of the bars. That's exactly what I did and once I worked my way to the top I had them pull around to the other side to meet me. The water wasn't as rough over there because the waves were slamming into the other side.

I wasn't going to pass up the opportunity to jump off this thing. I must have been fifty feet above the water and who knew what was going on beneath the surface. The water was so murky that your hand would disappear if you stuck it in over the side of the boat. Needless to say, I was fine and it was fun. It was time to stop fooling around and get this little craft over to the other side.

Once we made it to Crisfield, I quickly realized that Mike wasn't the partner that I wanted to have around. It turned out that, at the time, he had a drinking problem that I was unaware of prior to meeting him. I believe a man can do as he wishes, within reason, but he couldn't control himself. I even had a few beers but he was showing out, being rude, and even had the cops called. This wasn't the type of behavior I wanted to be associated with so we had to part ways. He went back home and I continued on solo.

I was a little upset since my original plan was to backpack across America and nearly all of my money had been sunk into this bike. I didn't let it bother me too much, though. I could always walk later if I wanted. So, with a positive outlook, I made my way into Delaware.

I ended the first night of my cross-country trek in Delmar. That's right on the state line with Maryland and Delaware. I looked around for a place to camp but I couldn't find a good spot.

This is also something that takes some getting used to. I eventually found a store that sells small sheds. I pulled my bike inside and put my sleeping bag down on the floor. This will work fine for tonight! That's what I thought anyways.

I was lying there for about an hour or so when I heard several cars pull up. It sounded like a group of teenagers and they were all playing loud music and screaming. I waited around for about another hour to see if they would leave but they seemed set on staying for a while. I was ready to go to sleep so I packed my things back up and got out of there.

There was no shoulder to ride on, it was dark, and it was raining. I didn't want to risk getting hit by a car so I began pushing my bike. I was almost out of town when I passed by a motel. There was a man standing outside and he yelled at me to come over.

He asked me what I was doing out there walking my bike in the rain. After I told him what I was up to he offered to pay for me a motel room for the night. The man working at the motel seemed to be dumbfounded by what he was witnessing. I got me a room, though, and thanked the man for his kindness.

The next morning, I mounted my bike, ready to take off, when I realized that I already had my first flat. I wasn't expecting this to happen so soon but I was prepared for it. I wasn't fast at changing a flat yet but I would get plenty of practice.

It wasn't much longer and I had claimed my Delaware sign. That became somewhat of a hobby of mine; collecting pictures of state signs as I made my way across America. I'm not sure if I'd call it a hobby exactly, but it was something to keep me motivated. You've got to have some kind of motivation to do anything and, for now, that was enough to keep me going.

Before making my way into Delaware I had switched our blog's name from "Jake and Mike Do America" to "Jake Does America". It just wouldn't make any sense to keep the old name if I was doing it by myself. A lot of Mike's friends and family were following the blog, though. When they found out that it was just me doing it they all gave me their two cents and excused themselves from my existence. No skin off my nose. They hadn't seen the side of him that I had seen.

Delaware sure was flat. I flew through there in a few hours and made my way into Pennsylvania. As soon as I crossed the state line it seemed like I was riding uphill forever. It was much more physically demanding than I had anticipated but it had a beauty to it that gave the hard work it's worth. Once I finally made it to a plateau there were green meadows that rolled on as far as I could see. Meadows, barns, and windmills. There wasn't much else going on out this way. It was quite peaceful.

I eventually passed through several Amish communities which I did not expect. As I passed by, they would run out to the street to offer me food and water. It was nice to be in an area where so many people would lend a hand to a complete stranger. Most of the time I had everything taken care of but it was their generosity that mattered.

It was quite obvious that I was raising some curiosity amongst the communities. The children were especially curious. They acted as though they had never seen someone traveling through with a bike loaded down with gear. I was equally curious about their hand-crafted, wooden scooters, though. I wouldn't mind watching them build one of those!

I decided I would head up to highway 30 (Lincoln Memorial Highway) and follow that west for a while. It would be easier to follow a coast to coast highway instead of zigzagging all over the place. That is what I ended up doing but it was something to focus on for now and I'm glad I did. Highway 30 certainly offered some interesting sites and people.

A couple of days later I stopped at a restaurant in Lancaster so I could eat on something other than dried noodles or trail mix. The waitress there, Dianna, was really nice. We talked while I was eating my burger and fries. She was intrigued by what I was doing and offered to pay for my lunch. She also sent me off with a huge bag of peanuts and we've been pretty good friends ever since.

A few hours after leaving Lancaster I found myself in Gettysburg. I rode up into the park and checked out all of the monuments. There wasn't a whole lot to look at but knowing the history of the area gave a dark feel to it. I've heard stories of Gettysburg being haunted which made me want to camp there. Too bad I didn't because I'd really like to see for myself!

After checking out of Gettysburg I was confronted by a mountain range that lasted all the way until about Pittsburgh. For four days straight, I completed two mountains each day. It doesn't sound like a lot but it was taking me a while to get through there.

Coming across a black bear really helped speed things up, though! I was coming up a mountain in the Buchanan State Forest when I saw the bear. I was tempted to turn around and go back down the mountain but I was too close to the top, and it had shown no interest in me. I sat and waited for the furry fellow to scurry back off into the woods.

I made it to the top of that mountain and it was

starting to get late. Since I had just seen a bear in the area it did raise a few concerns. I picked up the pace until I felt like I had found a good spot to camp. I wasn't too worried about that bear but I wanted to put some distance between us.

I finally found a sign that directed me towards a campground. When I arrived at the campground I discovered that it no longer existed. I had sidetracked fifteen miles to find a bar.

I made my way back to the highway and continued west until I came across a 4-H camp. It was closed at the time so I decided to take advantage of it. I made it just as it was getting dark. I made my way back to a small pond and set up my tent, ate a pack of crackers, and then it was off to sleep for me.

The next day I made my way to and through Pittsburgh. I didn't care to spend any time here. It just wasn't for me. I hadn't had enough stealth camping experience for a big city yet. I was walking my bike down one of the sidewalks, before I realized that you can ride with the traffic, and I was stopped by a group of guys. I guess my bike caught their attention and one of them asked where I was heading. I told him that I was making my way across the country and all of the guys got a kick out of it. They thought it was cool enough that they wanted me to get a picture of them and put it on my blog, so I did.

After making my way through Pittsburgh I ended up camping somewhere in the Racoon Creek State Park which was really laid back. They have a campground here but I stayed pretty far from all of that. Peace and quiet was what I needed after working my way through a busy city. I also had my first fire of the trip here and it made for some pretty good company. The fire was for more than entertainment, though. I had spent a couple of hours fishing as the sun was going down. Nothing puts me to sleep like a full stomach, listening to the coyotes, and the sound of a fire crackling. Tomorrow I'd be crossing the Ohio River.

The next morning, I had made a few miles before reaching West Virginia. It was a surprise to me because I hadn't noticed there was a small section of the state before crossing into Ohio. I stopped at a gas station before crossing the river because I wanted to make sure that I hadn't somehow got myself turned around somewhere. I was assured that I was in Chester, West Virginia.

There were a few sites to be seen here. There was a large blue house with a blue mannequin sitting on the front porch, a large statue of a boy playing a trumpet, the "World's Largest Teapot" that was furnished with a stove, couch, and table, and a sign that simply read "From This Sign You Are Exactly 1/4 The Way Around The World From Greenwich, England." A handful of neat and random things I'd never known existed otherwise.

I crossed the Ohio River and began towards Toledo. I was originally heading up to Findlay so I could meet up with a girl I had been talking to, but I decided against it. I didn't want to get caught up in any feelings because it could hinder what I was doing. I passed through Findlay and made my way to Lake Eerie at Luna Pier, Michigan. It took me about three days to get there but it was quite uneventful. Just a lot of riding and finding places to squat in the woods.

It was lunch time when I got there. I decided to go ahead and take the rest of the day off. I just wanted to enjoy the lake. I found a nice place to set up camp, caught me a couple of fish, and called it a night. The sound of the lake helped put me to sleep. I wanted to stay for a few days but I didn't want to get lazy. I had worked hard to build up my speed and stamina. I didn't want to lose that so no long breaks for me. Not yet anyways. Tomorrow I would be heading for Indiana.

I've noted a few times that I had caught some fish for dinner but I never said anything about having fishing poles. That was one of the several times where my training had come into play. When you are down on cash and nowhere near a store you had best have a backup plan. You will find all kinds of things on the road. If I planned on fishing that day I would keep my eye out for an aluminum can.

If you're unable to find a can, or at least a tab, sitting on the side of the road, then you are having some terrible luck. I would rip the cans apart and make little hooks. They were more like a barbed mess but if you mess around I'm sure you will figure something out. You can also start a fire with an aluminum can if you don't mind starting your fires in the day time. I was always trying to keep myself hidden, though. I would only start a day time fire if it was an emergency.

The next day I headed back down into Ohio and made it to Greenville by that night. I'd gather up whatever I needed here in the morning and be on my way into Indiana. It should be a breeze for a while now. The weather was cooling off and the land had begun to level out.

I packed up and crossed over into Indiana. Before the sun had set I had already made it into Terre Haute. This would be my last town in Indiana. I can't believe I had made it through an entire state in one day! Not that Indiana is a very large state but it felt like a huge accomplishment.

That was a bitter sweet feeling. I'm sure there was plenty to see but I was in the mood for speed. I kind of wanted to test myself because I was feeling stronger and faster. However, since I did this, I don't have much to say about Indiana; except for the fact that it's easy to ride a bike through.

You can probably imagine my face right now as I'm writing this. It's quite humorous when you take into consideration that I'm writing a book about my travels and have nothing to say about an entire state. Anyways, tomorrow I'll be making my way into Illinois.

A couple of hours after sunrise and I had made it into Illinois. The heat had returned and it slowed me down. I didn't mind slowing down, though, since I had just blown through Indiana. It wasn't long before I had taken refuge inside of a restaurant. I would have a slice of pizza and a beer for lunch while I waited for the sun to back off a bit. I didn't have the patience to wait until dark but I wanted to at least lower my risk of having a heat stroke.

I carried on after lunch and made my way into Effingham. It had been dark for about an hour before I got there. I was able to take a road that was beside the highway so I wouldn't have to worry so much about being ran over.

Once I got into town I sat outside of a gas station to charge my phone and MP3 player. It was getting late, I was in the middle of town, and I had no idea where to sleep. It was about 10:00 p.m. when the manager came out and asked me to leave.

I haven't mentioned it yet but that happened a lot. It's hard to find an outlet without people chasing you away from it. Even if I offered to pay for it they would still tell me to get lost. It wouldn't be long before I invested in a solar panel but for now it was time to find a place to sleep.

I made my way across the street and slept behind a military monument. It felt like an appropriate place for a veteran to get some rest. A storm moved in that night, though, and I was unable to put my tent up. It rained until morning so I wasn't able to get much sleep. I would have put my tent up if I could have found a spot but if I had done that here the police would have seen it, and most likely I would have had to take it down and be forced to leave.

Before the sun had even peeked over the horizon, I had packed up my soaking wet sleeping bag and made my way back over to the gas station. I was going to need some coffee for today. That was a rough night and my mind wasn't all there. It had been several years since I had to exert myself for days at a time. I would get back into the swing of things eventually. It's just kind of hard getting to that point.

I decided to head south to get down to highway 50. It didn't take long for me to realize that I was on highway 45, which led straight to my hometown. I could be there in two days if I wanted to. It crossed my mind but I had nothing to go back to. Even if I did, I knew that I would hate the feeling of giving up.

I had been of the road for a couple of weeks now and the loneliness was starting to get to me. Once I made it to highway 50 I sat at the intersection and stared down highway 45. I thought about heading home but I shook my head, let out a sigh, and made my way into St. Louis, Missouri.

Another state down and I was feeling pretty good. The fact that I turned down my chance to head home made me feel stronger. I'd make my way from St. Louis to St. Charles today. This is when I found out about the Katy Trail. It's an old railroad path that would take me all the way into Kansas. I wasn't aware of the trail until someone suggested it and I'm glad they did. A break away from all of the traffic would be nice.

From beginning to end, the Katy Trail was a calm and leisurely ride. There were several great spots to stop and just take it all in. Some of it was paved but most of it was dirt, and you never knew what would be around the next corner. I really enjoyed the sections where it ran along the Missouri River. I was in no hurry to get through this part of my trek but I did have somewhat of a schedule. I just needed to make it to one of the campgrounds before dark.

The only campground that I needed to stop at was really nice. There was a refrigerator full of snacks and drinks. There was no one there to take my money for the stuff, though; just a money box. They must have a lot of trust in the people who come through. I grabbed me a bag of chips and a drink, slipped a five-dollar bill into the box, and made my way to the campground area in the back. I was hoping for some company but I was the only one there on this lovely night. It was just me, the coyotes, and a nice little fire again.

The next day I continued on, enjoying the views that the trail had to offer. At some point the trail passed by a small town. I can't remember what town it was because I didn't actually go into it. I just stopped at an outdoor festival that was going on right off of the trail. I grabbed me a burger and beer for lunch which was offered to me for free by the cook. I must have been looking pretty rough at this point. When people start giving you stuff, including weird looks, you have to consider the fact that it might be time to try and get yourself cleaned up a bit!

I had been on the trail for a couple of days and decided that I'd get off in Jefferson City so I could continue into Kansas via highway 50. It was dark when I got into Jefferson City and I didn't know where I'd sleep for the night. I ended up choosing a silly place but I didn't know options were. I found a group of trees that were circled by one of the interstate exits. No fire tonight but it worked out great for a pit stop.

The next morning a man saw me packing up and leaving from my little spot in the bushes. He yelled at me to come over to the restaurant that was just across the exit ramp. When I got over to him he asked what I was doing. When I told him what I was up to he offered to buy me some breakfast. I was really grateful for his kindness. I was running low on cash and it got pretty chilly that night. A warm breakfast was definitely a good boost to get me into Kansas.

As I was coming into Kansas City I was contacted by a man named Greg. He was an older man who was into cycling and said that I could crash at his place if I wanted. He had been following my blog since I started and I guess I seemed innocent enough. He was the first person to offer me into their home. I took him up on his offer and I'm really glad that I did.

When I got to Greg's house he showed me around. It was kind of late when we got there and all I really cared about was a shower and some sleep, but he insisted on showing me his train collection. It was really neat the way he had it all set up. The whole basement was like a little town with the trains running through it. His wife finally told him to let me get a shower while they prepared supper. Both of those things sounded great to me!

The next day they offered to take me to the zoo. They had noticed from my blog that I had tried to stop at a few zoos but was forced to leave since they had nowhere to keep my bike. That was really cool of them! We spent a few hours walking around before I started to feel bad for all of the animals. I ended up having a panic attack so we left. I didn't tell them why I had the panic attack because I didn't want them to feel like they had wasted their money. I hadn't been to a zoo since I was a little kid. I had no idea that it was going to bother me.

After we left the zoo they took me by one of their favorite bike shops so I could get a maintenance check. It turned out that a few spokes had busted through both of my rims. How I had made it this far was a mystery to all of us so they had them replaced!

It had been a long day and returning to Greg's house for one more night felt like a great idea. I got another shower and then we ate dinner and watched a movie. We had spaghetti with garlic bread and pumpkin pie for dessert. Then it was off to bed for me. They let me sleep in a spare room that their grandchild used when he would visit.

The room looked like a kid's room. I almost felt like a kid sleeping in there. Tomorrow Greg would drop me off at the end of town on his way to work. It was somewhat necessary because it was an interstate and there were no pedestrians allowed. It was a great visit but it was time to be moving on.

From Kansas, I went down to Oklahoma until I hit highway 60 in Ponca City. I hate to skip so much but there really wasn't much out that way. It was a whole lot of nothing. As little as there is to talk about, it was quite nice. The weather was really starting to cool off and the roads were mostly mine. The drivers that occasionally did pass weren't like the ones before. People began to slow down and give me strange looks, probably wondering what a person was doing out here in the middle of nowhere on a bicycle.

Before we move on from here I have to mention The Rolling Hills in Kansas. The hills were like a green ocean with the wind giving them the life of a spirited dancer. There weren't very many trees anymore. Just a fair number of shrubs.

The trees that I did see looked baron, like they had survived a number of tornadoes; such as the one that barely missed me while I was camping underneath a gazebo at a rest stop. I can't remember where I was exactly when that happened but it was a scary experience.

By the time I had reached Texas I had been on the move for a month. The loneliness and lack of finances was really starting to get to me. I knew I could survive off of the land if I had to but there are a lot of legal issues to worry about should it came to that.

I decided that it would be wiser to begin dumpster diving. That's a sad but true statement, and besides my lack of money for food, it was beginning to get really cold at night. Even though I was layering up and using my cell phone to produce extra heat, my forty-degree sleeping bag just wasn't enough to keep me warm anymore.

I made it into Amarillo before I felt like I was in any serious trouble as far as my health goes. My body was no longer agreeing with the weather. I'm sure I could have made something to keep me going but I wasn't in a very good state of mind. My depression was returning and I was down on my luck. The sun went fast and it was another cold night stuck in the city.

I was surrounded by drug addicts who were roaming the streets. At one point, I tried sleeping at a park but I got out of there after I saw a drug deal. I went across the street and slept up against the wall of a McDonald's. The next morning, I went in to sit down and warm up. I needed to come up with a way to keep warm at night and to make notes for my route so I didn't end up in any more cities after dark.

While I was sitting there a man came up and offered to have breakfast with me. Sam was his name. We sat and talked for a while before he got up to leave. I was still sitting there so I could charge my things when Sam returned. He handed me a wad of cash and wished me luck. I thanked him for his help and after he left I counted out three hundred dollars! That was such a huge help! The fact that it came from a complete stranger really blew my mind. Now that I had this money I could make some changes to my situation.

I thought about the conversation I had with Sam and decided that I would give my bike to a homeless man. I walked downtown and got a bus ticket back home. I felt like I'd had enough and going to visit my family would probably be for the best. As I was waiting for my bus to arrive I wondered if I had made a mistake but I couldn't think of anything that would change my mind.

I boarded the bus and headed back for Tennessee. As I was watching everything pass me in reverse I began to feel like I had failed. It was a mixture of emotions but what was done was done. I wasn't physically or mentally prepared to continue. I'm having a tough time explaining how bad I was actually feeling but going back was probably the best idea. I really had to thank Sam for this opportunity to go back and try to do everything the right way.

Once I made it back to Tennessee I was still homeless

but I found a job in Martin. I was working with people who were mentally challenged. It was a really fun job. No one had any idea that I was homeless, though. I hid it pretty well I guess.

I had my tent set up off in the woods behind a gas station and would clean up in their bathroom every morning before work. It seemed like everything was beginning to fall back into place for me. I was saving all of my money so I would be able to get a vehicle and live in it until I could afford an apartment. I was working my way back up from rock bottom.

I ended up falling in love again. Man, I sure am a sap for that stuff huh? Before I could use that money for a car me and this girl ended up renting a house down the road from where I was working. She had a car and let me use it if I needed to but I rarely did. Work was within walking distance and she needed it for work too. Walking obviously wasn't an issue for me. Everything seemed to be coming together pretty well. Life was simple, I was happy, and it felt like a dream come true. Like they say, though, if it's too good to be true then it probably is.

One day I had a severe panic attack at work and it cost me my job. The supervisor was really nice and understanding. He tried talking to me and wanted to give me a chance at staying with them. It wasn't the end of the world for needing a break from work for a couple of days but I felt like a complete failure. I was too ashamed of myself for having a panic attack.

My panic attack lead to depression and soon after that my girlfriend decided she wanted to part ways. We put the lease to the house in her name and I was homeless again. Homeless, alone, and depressed. What in the world? Why does everything keep coming crashing down?

I tried my best to keep my head up. I still had some money saved at least and had been seeing a psychiatrist for a couple of months. He was able to help me get an apartment for people with mental disorders. I guess because I was homeless it helped to speed things along, too.

I had to bring in papers to the apartment owners that proved that I had bipolar and post-traumatic stress disorder. It took about a week and I was approved to move in. It was a bit weird living in an apartment complex specifically for people with mental disorders. Everyone knew this was the place where the "crazies" lived so there was a stigma tied to just being there.

Everyone here pretty much stuck to themselves, though. That was great. I just wanted to be left alone anyways. An added bonus was that it was only $100 a month to live here (utilities included) so I could make this work! I had enough money to get a computer and a few other things so I could pick back up with audio engineering, and be able to pay my bills.

It was December of 2013 when I moved in and by March, 2014 I had already made enough money to get a car and have my apartment completely furnished. Not too bad for working from home on my own time! I spent that summer sitting in my apartment racking up money to buy all of these things that I thought I wanted; things that I thought would make me happy.

It actually doesn't sound like that bad of a gig, does it? It really wasn't. But I wasn't happy and there's nothing more important than that. Happiness is not something you can put a price on. What I am about to do made me feel a bit selfish and disrespectful to the people who had given me this opportunity, but here I go again.

I needed some kind of purpose in life. Screw what these people think of me. Screw everything. There was something bigger out there for me and I knew it. I could make a difference and all I needed was my own two feet.

2

I put everything I had up for sale. My car, my computer, my furniture. Everything was gone. I just wanted enough money to get me started on my next journey. I wasn't sure what it was yet but I knew it would come to me. I knew that whatever was going to happen wasn't going to happen unless I made the change.

It took me about a week to sell most of the things in my apartment. My home was looking almost as blank as the day I moved in. Only a few small items remained so I decided to sit them outside in some boxes. The next morning everything was gone.

I made my way to the library just as I had done before and ordered a new bike with all the extras to go with it. I was able to get everything that I would need. I had about $5,000 to start this time so I was able to get some better gear, which made a substantial difference.

Everything arrives a few days later and I piece it all together. No one knows what's going on in here in my apartment. I was doing it all on my own and no one had any idea or say in it.

I slept next to my loaded bike that night and wondered where I would go from here. That's right. I had no idea where I was even going or why. During the night, it hit me that my best friend was living in Foley, Alabama so I would head down there. That was the plan for now. Nothing more and nothing less.

The next morning, I pulled my bike out and walked over to my landlord. I handed her the key to my apartment and said, "Thanks for letting me stay here."

She had a confused look on her face. I didn't say anything else. She may have said something but I wasn't paying attention. I positioned my bike south and took off. Easy as that.

It was August 15th, 2014 when I left my hometown again. Another balmy day to start and it was only about to get worse. I knew that this was going to be a miserable start but I was ready for it. I made it to Selmer, Tennessee by the end of my first day back at it. Ninety-three miles wasn't too bad for being out of commission for almost a year.

That first night back out in my tent felt great except for the heat radiating off of my face. Maybe I wasn't as prepared as I thought. I had forgotten to pack some sunscreen and out here it was a necessity. I've tried cycling with hats on before but I could never get one to stay on my head. Since I was heading south the sun would be in my face all day. There is no shade out on highway 45 unless you can make it to an overpass and I can only recall three of those.

A couple of hours after I had set up camp, something woke me up while it was making its way through the brush that I had used for cover. I popped my head out to find an armadillo checking my tent out. It wasn't scared of me in the least bit. I figured the sound of the zipper would have whatever it was running for its life, but not this guy.

I decided to reach into my saddle bag and find something I could share with him. We sat there and shared a can of chips until he was licking the crumbs up off of the ground. That was a good way to end both of our nights.

Tomorrow I'd be making my way through Mississippi.

I made it into Corinth, MS before noon and decided to go ahead and give my clothes a wash. Yesterday's sweat had dried and made my clothes feel stiff. If I didn't swap my pairs out regularly they would be worn out in no time; that and I'd end up with a rash more difficult to get rid of than a hungry armadillo.

You're probably wondering why I'd even mention having to do laundry. I had to keep clean somehow and that was a question that I got asked quite frequently. Sometimes I would bathe and do laundry in creeks but I would work with whatever I had. Most of the time, like today, I would find myself in a public restroom to take care of my hygienic needs.

Having to carry a bag of clothes into a gas station restroom is a little embarrassing, but it worked well if you could get over that. This time was a bit more memorable, though. I guess I only remember it better this time because I stopped caring after that.

It became casual for me as time went on, but this time while I was in the parking lot wringing out my clothes, the manager came outside. He never said anything. He was just standing there with his arms crossed; watching me like I had just broken the law. I wouldn't have been surprised if he had called the cops. That did end up happening a few times.

Another day in the sun had gone by and I was ending my day south of Tupelo. Tonight, I found myself camping underneath a bridge. It seemed like a good spot until I was awakened by the sound of a group of partying teenagers. Luckily for me, they never came up over the hill where I was at. I didn't know them or feel like dealing with anyone. I was exhausted and just wanted some sleep. It seemed like everywhere I went there was something that came to visit me in the night.

The next day was probably the hottest I'd push myself through. It was the longest ride without any shade, too. I felt like I was on the verge of a heat stroke a couple of times. I ran out of water a couple of times, too, but I was able to find a place to fill up before it was too late.

I began to think that a bike was the best choice I'd made because walking out here would have meant the end of me. Tomorrow I'll be crossing into Alabama. I had a friend on the other side of Mobile. I hadn't seen her in a while so that was my motivation for now.

Day five back at it was another scorcher but it would get easier since there were more towns coming up. After I crossed the Alabama state line I had been out of water for a few hours. Luckily, I spotted a church with a water spigot on the side of it.

I went over to fill up and completely drenched myself. Actually, I turned it on and just laid underneath it for a few minutes. A truck that had passed by earlier that day saw me and stopped to see if everything was going okay. If he had stopped before I noticed that church with running water I would have given him a big fat "no", but all was well. I did appreciate his concern, though.

I pushed my way on into Mobile and got out of there as quickly as I came. A huge storm approached just as I was making my way across the bridge over the bay. The rain gave me the boost that I needed to make it down to Foley. That's where my friend, Sydney, was living at the time. I called to let her know I'd be there in a few hours. She was as surprised as I was. Five hundred miles in five days. Not bad!

I met up with Sydney at the Walmart in Foley. We hung out there while we were waiting for a taxi back to her place. It felt good to see a friend that I hadn't seen in a while. I could feel my energy being restored because I knew we were about to be into all kinds of fun. She and me go pretty far back and we were well-known to be a handful.

After we left the store we made our way to where she was staying so I could drop off my things. Then we made our way down to Orange Beach to have a few beers and take a swim in the Gulf of Mexico. I'd never been to the beach before. I'd been to a lot of places, but not the beach. We were having a blast and it was easy for her to convince me to stay here for a while.

The next day we pretty much picked up where we left off. She took me to a bar where she was working so I could meet her new friends. They all thought that it was crazy that I just rode a bike down from Tennessee and offered me some free drinks. Everything felt like it was going right. I could see myself sticking around here.

That same night everything would change, though. We carried a few beers down to the beach again. This time I was well-rested and ready to play. We knew that we shouldn't be in the gulf after dark since that's when the dangerous marine animals come close to shore. We didn't leave until I was stung by a school of jellyfish. I'm not sure if urine helps or not but it will take your mind off of the pain. Thanks, Sydney!

It had to be about 11:00 pm now and we decided to make our way back to her apartment. Before heading back home she wanted to walk over to the hotel where one of her friends was working. We stopped at a gas station across from the hotel so she could grab a sandwich and a few other snacks. After we left the gas station she swung over to my left side and began eating her sandwich. We continued towards the hotel.

We were making our way across the street when I noticed a car coming from the right, but the left side was clear. There weren't any turns here so I walked to the median where I would stop and wait for the car to pass. Sydney was only paying attention to her sandwich, though.

As the car approached, I looked over to notice that Sydney hadn't stopped. She must have assumed that since I was walking, it must have been safe to cross. Since she was on the left, she wouldn't have been able to see the car coming from my side. My heart stopped. I saw the accident coming and there was nothing I could do about it.

She almost made it across, which is something we both would have joked about, but she got hit. The car was probably going about 20 miles per hour when it struck her. She went flying into the hotel's driveway and I was sure she was dead. I ran up to her and began screaming her name because she was unconscious.

The lady who was driving got out and called 911 so I kept my focus on Sydney. She wasn't dead but she was seriously injured. When I first saw her open her mouth I thought she had suffered serious head trauma, but it was only the sandwich; and she was still trying to chew it. She had no idea that she had even been hit.

The medics arrived and we were both taken to the hospital in Pensacola, Florida. She was going to be okay but she had several broken bones. I stayed in the hospital with her for a few days until she was released under the care of her parents. Her parents took her back to Tennessee where she would have to undergo several months of therapy. I didn't know what I was going to do now but least Sydney was okay!

One of Sydney's family members brought me back to Sydney's apartment so I could get my bike. After that I didn't really know what I was doing. I just started riding. I decided that I would stick close to the beach while I waited for the weather to cool off and then I would make my way for Alaska. I've always wanted to see Alaska!

As I was riding deeper into Florida that night I posted on my blog about what had happened. It turned out that my aunt and uncle lived just a couple of hours away. My uncle came to pick me up and said I could stay with them in Ft. Walton Beach, FL until the heat subsided.

I stayed with my uncle for the next month but most of my time here was be spent bumming it at the beach. Nothing wrong with that! I had nothing but time to kill and what better way than sitting at the beach, taking it easy. Okay, it sounds great and all, but it gets old pretty quick. Most people could probably hang out at the beach longer than I could. It was nice to see my family and get to chill out near the ocean, but now I can't focus on much other than getting to Alaska.

It sounds like a very impulsive idea to just up and go to Alaska, especially when you're on the completely opposite side of the country; not to forget to mention Canada in between. But it really had been a place that I'd always wanted to see. I've always been fascinated by the idea of living there, out in the bush on my own and away from everyone.

I made an attempt to leave Florida on September 1st but it was still too hot. I rode about 50 miles north when I realized that I was sweating more than I could drink. I don't think I had ever sweat that much! I would have to head back down and wait another week or two before I could get out of there. The heat was still just too dangerous. I couldn't believe that I made it through Mississippi to be honest. I didn't want to test myself like that again!

A couple more weeks in Florida was enough time for me to give my journey some meaning. I decided that I would raise some money while I was at it. I just needed to find a good charity of choice. I looked around for a few and I went with Shot At Life. They had an application for my phone where they could keep track of my miles and since I had so many ahead of me it seemed like a good choice.

I decided to head north before going west. The days were still too hot out in the mid-western states. At the rate I was going, it would still be that way when I got there. I figured it would be best to find a way to make some time until it cooled off.

It didn't take long for fall to come as I was making my way north. It was comfortable again and I could get nearly two hundred miles down if I wanted to. I tried to take in more of my surroundings this time, though. Some days were faster than others. I'd pick a spot on my map that looked interesting and make it there as soon as possible so I could take the time to enjoy it. After fighting my way through millions of ants (every morning for the first week I would wake up with my saddle bags covered with them), I had made my way just south of Columbus, Georgia.

I didn't plan on going into Columbus but I wanted my Georgia sign. I needed to stock up on food and water first, though. Luckily, I came across a Dollar General Store. The manager here talked to me for a few minutes and offered to purchase my food for me. He even let me use the microwave in the back so I could heat up a pizza. Before I left he even handed me $20!

I headed back into Alabama from here and made my way towards Lake Martin. I was always on the lookout for lakes and parks. This just happened to be one of them. There was a campsite here where I had decided to stop and stay for two days before moving on. It was too cold for a swim but I got in for a quick wash. The cold water was great for my sore muscles. From here I would make my way to Talladega National Forest.

I didn't go too far into Talladega National Forest but I found me a great spot on top of a hill, which offered a relaxing view of the sunset. A storm came through later that night, though, which meant that a cold front was on the way. After spending so much time outside you can pretty much tell what the weather is going to do. It's just something that you get used to. It's like a basic instinct that returns after some time.

After I woke up in the Talladega National Forest I climbed out of my tent to feel the nice cool breeze. I immediately noticed a dry spot in front of my tent. The rain had stopped about an hour before I got up and it started as soon as I laid down the night before.

Did something come and spend the night next to me? It was an oddly shaped dry spot about the size of my tent. I thought this was strange because I never heard anything and I am a very light sleeper. I was curious but there was nothing I could do to figure out what it was. No branches overhead and no tracks. I shrugged it off and made myself a cup of coffee and oatmeal before heading out.

On my way it into Huntsville, I was confronted by a set of mountains. No big deal except for the fact that there was a tornado headed my way. If I could make it to the top in time, I would be able to coast down the other side; out of the storm's path. With no time to spare, I got a flat about halfway up the mountain. I could see the storm approaching and it was picking up strength. Just my luck!

It took me about fifteen minutes to fix my flat but before I could get moving the rain had begun to fall. I was hoping I could still beat the storm to the top. I pedaled harder than I had before. My energy, however, was wasted. As soon as I made it to the top the storm was directly over me. If only I hadn't got that flat!

The top of a mountain, with nowhere to go, is not where you want to be when a storm hits. I know that you shouldn't get close to trees during a storm but I hunkered down next to a large oak. The rain was heavy and the wind was strong, but the lightning was my greatest fear. After getting caught in a situation like this there isn't much you can do except curse yourself for trying to beat a storm up a mountain. What was I thinking?

A tornado warning went off on my phone so I proceeded to get up and jump across the guard rail on the other side. It wouldn't help much but at least it was a bit lower than the side I was on. As soon as I began to walk towards the guard rail, though, lightning hit it. I decided I would just sit back down. Lightning was hitting everything and trees were snapping all around me. It was a very frightening thirty minutes that could have been avoided. Lesson learned? Don't gamble with mother nature!

I had made it back into Tennessee by the next morning and found my way into Murfreesboro. As I was coming into the city I came across a bike trail that had been closed due to flooding. I knew that the waters had receded back into the river so I made my way onto the trail.

I saw a cyclist heading in my direction and thought that he must have been a local and knew that the trail was safe to ride on. About a minute after he had passed I heard someone coming up behind me. It was the man that had just passed by. He pulled up beside me and asked, "Jake"? I gave him a confused look and asked if I knew him.

He said that he had seen one of my gear reviews online and was following my blog. How strange to run into a follower, especially on a trail that was closed!

He offered me to ride with him so I could stay the night at his house. It wasn't too far from the trail until we arrived at his home. It was a really nice neighborhood and he had done pretty good for himself, I'd say. Turns out that he and his wife were both teachers at the school there.

We sat around and mostly discussed cycling gear while waiting for his wife to get home. He then called his friend over to meet me so he could get in on the conversation, too. They were planning a cycling trip in another country. I can't remember where they were going but I gave them the best advice I could.

While we were out in their garage I pulled out most of my gear to show them what all I carried. I mostly talked about my Nashbar TR1 bike, Eureka Midori 2 tent, Counter Assault bear spray, and my SunTactics solar panel.

At some point, they asked me how effective the bear spray was. I told them about a time I had to use it on a large dog that wouldn't back off and how some of it came back at me with the wind. I had no doubt that it would deter a bear, or anything else for that matter.

The friend that he had called over asked me to give it a quick tap so they could get an idea of it. I shot a quick burst out of the garage door and the wind brought some back towards us. It was just as powerful as I remembered and it sent us all inside, coughing and agreeing that it was a worthy deterrent. I'm glad neither of them had asthma!

Once his wife was home she even mentioned that the garage smelled like peppers. We laughed because it had been about two hours since we had come back into the house. That's what happens when you get a couple of guys together, though!

Anyways, it was time for dinner and I was starving. Some kind of chicken pasta that tasted like it had fallen from heaven, at least to me anyways. After supper, I was able to jump into the shower. I tried to make it a short one as not to be rude but I accidentally used up all of their hot water. Whoops!

After I was out of the shower I was shown to the guest room. Holy smokes! It was like I had just entered a five-star hotel room! Maybe that was just because I hadn't slept in a bed in a while but I'll tell you I sure felt out of place. I was asleep as soon as I hit the bed. Tomorrow I'd be making my way into Nashville.

After leaving the teachers' house it only took a couple of hours to make it into Nashville. I remembered watching the weather at their house and tonight was forecast to be pretty bad. I didn't want to get caught up in the storms outside of the city so I hung out at a park. I wasn't there long before the news crew arrived to broadcast the weather that was approaching. I knew it was going to be a long night.

Darkness came earlier than usual since there was a super cell storm making its way in. Luckily, there was a hotel nearby that I could take cover in. I brought my bike into the lobby and took a seat. People were running in off the streets to get out of the storm just as I had done. The manager came and told everyone they had to leave because the hotel was for guests only.

I was really shocked that they would make people leave but at least they had other places to go. Good thing he didn't notice me! Or maybe he did but assumed that I was a guest. I was trying to fit in with the crowd so I made a cup of coffee and watched the weather channel. I guess it worked!

Eventually, this older man came over and started talking to me. Not to offend deceased actor, Sir Alec Guinness, but that's who he reminded me of (physically anyways). He began comparing me to his boyfriend and saying how he would rather have me than him. Yeah, this was really awkward! He went up to his room and said he would be back in a few minutes. I took that time to get out of there. I'd take my chance with the storm!

It was a lot worse than I had thought. A few tornadoes had touched down in the surrounding area and, according to the weather map, it looked likely to happen again. I decided to find a cheap motel for the night. I accidentally chose a rough neighborhood for a motel room, the same one where the movie "The Thing Called Love" was shot, but at least I was out of the elements. My tent has proved itself time and time again but I would feel safer behind some solid walls; or at least a roof over my head. Mostly for protection from the lightning. That was my greatest concern.

The next morning, I began heading east. I was making too good of time and figured I'd make a loop to give the season a little more time to change. As I made my way into the mountains of the Catoosa Wildlife Area I was confronted by a man who was taking pictures of the scenery. He asked me what I was doing and I told him that I was trekking from Florida to Alaska. He laughed and said that I was going the wrong way if I was trying to get to Alaska. He took my picture, though. I'm not sure why he took my picture if he didn't have any faith in me. Maybe it was in case I came up missing. Who knows?

A few hours later and I had made my way into Oak Ridge. I had a couple of friends here that said I could stay the night with them. I took the offer and headed over to their house. When I got there, Bee and her husband Andrew welcomed me into their home. I was greeted with a large bowl of chili and a beer. After we ate they let me get a shower. I must admit that I was getting pretty lucky with all of these kind people! After I came back from my shower we sat around and talked about aliens until I passed out on the couch.

The next morning, I made my way into Knoxville so I could meet up with my friend, Rachael. I found a pair of three hundred dollar sunglasses and I figured she would probably like them. I found all kinds of things while traveling. Things that usually had no purpose to me but things that I could sell or trade.

I tried to pawn the sunglasses before bringing them to her but all of the pawnshops I stopped at thought that I had stolen them. I can't argue with that, though, because I looked like a bum; and these were really expensive sunglasses designed for women.

Rachael was busy with work and school when I got there so I decided that I would camp in Knoxville. I didn't mind taking a little break so I could see her the next morning. I got out of the inner city before looking for a place to camp but I didn't want to go too far. I spotted a church that had a car next to the side door so I made my way over. The door was unlocked so, after a few knocks, I let myself in.

I was walking around inside the church, trying to find someone. I wanted to ask for permission to camp in the back. Finally, an older lady came out of a room and she looked terrified. She immediately asked how I got in there.

I told her that the door was unlocked and that I was cycling across America for Wounded Warriors Project (I switched over to this charity once I made it into Tennessee). I asked if it would be okay for me to camp in the back and she said that it was fine.

It's better when you ask for permission. You don't have to be so paranoid about getting harassed by any police officers. Just make sure to get the person's name and number when you ask because the cops will want to know if they show up. This time was no exception. Right after I put my tent up, a couple of officers pulled around back and immediately came over to me. They jumped to conclusions and said I couldn't stay here but there was a homeless shelter downtown.

This actually happened a lot. People always tried directing me to homeless shelters until I told them what I was doing. The look on people's faces when I enlightened them was the best feeling.

The next morning, I met up with Rachael. She loved the sunglasses and gave me a kiss on the cheek. I'd say that was a fair trade! I didn't want those sunglasses but she was the type that was into things like that. We talked for about an hour before she had to be on her way to school.

She said that she was going to order me a zero-degree sleeping bag since the one I had was a forty-degree bag and winter was just around the corner. She never did, though. I don't think she thought I was going to make it all the way to Alaska. I can't blame her for that. It sounds like a crazy idea! I still appreciated her consideration, though.

After leaving Knoxville I made my way north for Kentucky. The last town on the state line was Jellico. I'd have to resupply there before crossing the state line. The night just before reaching town I slept behind another church that had some picnic tables in the back. A perfect place to eat my dinner and get some good rest.

I heard something knock over the steel trash can while I was asleep. I peeked my head out to find a bear digging around for scraps. I screamed at it to get out of there but it didn't run off like I expected it to. It slowly started to walk towards me. I remembered seeing a brick beside my tent before I crawled in for the night. With my bear spray in one hand, I took the brick and smacked it against a nearby air conditioner. Luckily, that got the bear out of there and I now knew to be more aware as I made my way into Daniel Boone National Forest!

The leaves were beginning to change colors, the days were getting shorter, and the hot days were well behind me. It was the perfect time to take a ride down some country back roads. I was riding along with a creek for most of the day. Since I had seen a bear the night before I was hoping to see another one, but I didn't. The water seemed to keep me company as I strolled along, though. It was a beautiful and calm day until I came up to field full of little orange balls.

The little orange balls turned out to be baby pumpkins. I couldn't tell what they were from the road so I went over to inspect them. After I realized they were pumpkins I had a good laugh. I should have known what they were but it took me by surprise. Not as surprising as what happened on my way back to my bike, though.

While I was walking back to the road I heard a gunshot come from a house that was across the street. Was someone trying to scare me away from their precious pumpkin patch? That's what I assumed until I noticed some smoke and the smell of an illegal substance. I knew what I had stumbled upon and I hopped on my bike to get out of there.

I heard a second gun shot, but this time I also heard shotgun pellets hitting the road around me. Man, I got out of there quick! I made it through the forest in one piece but not so much at peace anymore. Luckily, no one followed me out of there. I would have called the cops but I didn't have any cell service out there.

I had made it to the outskirts of Burnside when a white van pulled over. Classic, right? I've become used to people stopping to ask if I needed anything. I figured that's what this person was doing. Maybe he wanted to offer me a ride, water, food, or even a few bucks. All of that had become pretty much a daily thing but this man had a different idea.

I approached the van to see a large heavyset white man. He appeared to just be getting off of work as his hands and overalls were covered in paint. I assumed this must be his work van, and it probably was; but things were about to get weird.

At first, he asked me if I needed a ride, which I declined since I was doing this for charity. He then asked how I made money while I was traveling. I told him that I had some money in my bank account but I'd do odd jobs on the side if needed.

The man asked if I was looking to have some fun. I had my guard half choked because, who knew, maybe he just wanted to go fishing or something. So, I replied, "Maybe. What kind of fun are we talking about?" He went on to say that we could get a motel room and have a few drinks.

I've had people offer to rent me a motel room before but this man had something different in mind. He wasn't some guy looking to me help out. He was looking for a type of service that I was not interested in!

When I declined his offer, he asked me if I had a gun on me. Okay, things are starting to get a little edgy now so I told him that I did. He replied, "Oh, okay. I do too. You wouldn't want to be out here without one." I told him that's why I carry one (I didn't, but I wish I did at the time) and said that I'd best be on my way because I needed to get to the next town before dark.

I backed away from his van and proceeded to take out my cell phone. I aimed it at him to make him think I was taking his picture. He immediately sped off in the opposite direction. I got out of there just as fast as he did but I sure did keep my eye out for him until I made it to the next town. I didn't see him again, thankfully!

The next morning, I made my way into Bowling Green. It was a cold Sunday morning, and although I had my phone, I only knew it was Sunday because church was in session. I had stopped worrying about what day it was a long time ago, but I decided to stop at one of the churches to fill up on water. I wasn't the only one who had decided to fill up at this church, though. There were two other people sitting on the front steps, waiting for the church to serve meals to the homeless.

I decided to sit with them and try to have some normal conversation. A young male and an older female, both dressed in all black clothing. I didn't mind, of course, but the people at the church did. The guy, who went by the name Raven, said they were refused to enter because they looked like devil worshipers, but they could sit outside until they were ready to serve breakfast. It's sad to know people will treat others by the way they look, but it happens; and I knew it did all too well.

We had some funny conversations, though. It helped to elevate all of our moods. We laughed at how they would put people down for not having good enough clothes or vehicles to be welcomed into their church. It was funny to see them leave in a hurry, while cursing people who wouldn't get out of their way fast enough. People watching can be quite entertaining but I'd had enough. It was time for me to get going. I got my water and wished them well.

From Bowling Green, I would be heading for Land Between The Lakes on highway 79. This would bring me back down into Tennessee, to the place where I grew up doing a lot of fishing and camping. It felt nice to be here again, at the lake, and it was perfect weather for it. I hadn't been here in a while and everything was pretty much the same. I'd camp and fish here tonight. Tomorrow I'll probably head back to my hometown to visit my family one last time before continuing on to Alaska.

My parents were surprised to see me back again. They didn't know that my route had landed me back in town but home was a good place to gear up for winter, as well as see the doctor.

I had lost feeling in one of my hands and had signs of muscular dystrophy. It turned out that I had a crushed ulnar nerve from poor bike fitting. I decided to stay here for about a month. It was a safe place to let my hand heal and prepare for the winter ahead.

I refused to stay inside during my visit with my parents,

though. The woods would accommodate me just fine. I had already become used to staying outside and I didn't want to get that domesticated feeling again. It takes a couple of months to get used to living outdoors, as well as being alone most of the time.

So, that's what I did. I stayed in the woods behind their house, practicing my survival skills until Thanksgiving. Not a whole lot to talk about from my time spent here. Time flew buy pretty fast and after having Thanksgiving dinner with my family it was time to push on.

I was heading back into Memphis on the same route as before except this time I made it in one day instead of two. My speed and stamina had gone way up, and I felt great. This seemed like a good time to switch from riding for Wounded Warriors Project to mental health awareness. I had noticed a drastic change in myself and I wanted to show others the positive effect exercise, and being outdoors, had on your mental health.

I found out that Sydney was living in Memphis so I went to stay with her for two days. It was great seeing her again and how much she had recovered. She had a limp and some gnarly scars, but still the same old Sydney. She noted how much I had changed and I could feel it, too. I was dirty and wild, but a lot happier and healthier.

After hanging out with my old friend it was time to hit the road again. It was pretty late when I left Sydney's house, so when I got through Memphis it was beginning to get dark. The sun was setting as I was making my way across the bridge into Arkansas. I made it across and found me a place to camp for the night.

I'm glad that I had purchased some new winter gear before I left Tennessee. It was getting really cold now. My first night in Arkansas I slept back behind a mound of dirt that was piled up next to an auto repair shop. I couldn't pitch my tent because I needed to keep a low profile.

I laid my sleeping gear out on the ground and slept cozy but woke with everything covered in ice. It was cold enough that I had to take my knife and cut off all the mud that had accumulated on my tires from the night before.

I made it into Palestine in time for lunch. I pulled out a can of soup to find that it was frozen. It takes some time to eat a frozen can of soup. I had a solar panel, but the overcast made it pretty much useless.

I'd take the time here to find an outlet so I could charge my things and eat my frozen soup. Since the days were getting shorter, I would go ahead and end my night somewhere between here and Goodwin.

Once I made it to Brinkley I had about two hours of daylight left to make it through the wetlands. I made it through there pretty quick because I didn't want to be stuck out here with nowhere to escape from the road.

Of course, I would ride at night if I had to, but I tried to avoid it. I made it into Biscoe with some daylight to spare. I spotted a grocery store with some soda machines and made my way over to them. I don't know why, but after traveling for a while I started to crave sodas, even though I never used to drink them.

After I grabbed a drink, I made my way over to a baseball park that was just across the street. The sun was starting to set and there was rain closing in. I wanted to find me a good spot before it became too difficult to see.

I like to check out my surroundings before settling down, if possible. The baseball field hadn't been used in years so I felt pretty safe sleeping in the dugout. I saw a shed nearby and decided to go investigate.

People had been using the shed as a place to skin their deer and there was a fresh pile of guts thrown to the side; along with several bones. I looked around a bit more and found an old baseball trophy that had the same date as my birthday.

What were the chances in that! I wanted to keep it but I knew I'd eventually just toss it in the trash. I walked back to the dugout where I had left my bike and decided to take everything on the other side.

I didn't want to be anywhere near that rotting meat in case something decided to come chow down on it. From this side, though, I was visible from the road. I'd be better off pitching my tent between a group of trees. I picked up several branches to aid in my camouflage and settled in for the night.

It was another cold and wet morning as I was making my way through De Valls Bluff when a white truck pulled over. I noticed two men and a dog inside and figured they were probably going to offer me a ride; since that had happened several times. They didn't offer me a ride, though. They were just curious as to what I was up to. When I told them I was making my way to Alaska, they both said that I was living their dream, and wanted to get a picture with me.

I can't remember the passenger's name, but the man driving told me his name was Anthony. He handed me $20, shook my hand, and wished me well. He took off on his way to work and so did I. My work was just a little bit different. The money was always helpful but a few words of encouragement can get you a lot further.

I made it into Carlisle in time for lunch and then I'd be making my way into Little Rock. The highway turned into an interstate. I hate when that happens, but I hate it even more when the interstate turns into a bridge with no shoulder! I had no other choice but to weave my way in and out of traffic. What a headache that was!

I made it across the bridge into Little Rock just as it was getting dark and by the time I was downtown it was pitch black. I was debating on whether or not to push on through but I was feeling drained.

I was scurrying around to try and find a place to sleep. I'd never been in Little Rock before so I didn't know of any good spots. I could tell that I was in a bad part of town, though, and had to get out of here if I wanted any rest.

I was able to get out of the metropolitan area and

found my way into a rich neighborhood. Of course, I didn't know that at the time because I couldn't see anything. I found a side road that had several trees and thought that would be my best bet. I was too tired to put my tent up and figured I'd spend another night lying on the ground.

I was in my sleeping bag for about thirty minutes when I heard a car pull up. Then I heard a gate opening and noticed that the car was leaving. Now I realized that I was at the end of someone's driveway! Maybe everything would be okay, though. I felt like if they came back I'd be out of site and be gone before sunrise anyways.

I tried to get some sleep but after another thirty minutes, a bunch of lights came on. That's when I noticed that I was sleeping outside of a mansion!

A security guard then came and parked his car right beside me to watch over the gate. Man, if I get caught here they would probably suspect I was trying to rob them or something. The security guard got out of his vehicle and walked around to do an inspection. He walked right by me without noticing.

He went back to his vehicle and I decided I'd better get while the getting was good. I slid out of my sleeping bag and tucked everything back into my saddle bags. Now, how was I going to get me and my bike out of there without this guard seeing me?

I quietly walked my bike a little further back, maybe twenty feet, until I reached a fence. I followed along the fence until I noticed a low spot in it and tossed my bike over. I pushed my bike back down to the road and got out of there.

I didn't want to ride at night but I felt like I had no other option. I made my way back to highway 70 to do a few miles out of town. I probably rode for a mile when I nearly got hit in the eye by a rock. That was a good sign for me to stop and find a place to sleep. I was finally out of Little Rock and made my way into a wooded area.

The next morning I'd take some back roads until I made it to Hot Springs. I was tired of dealing with so much traffic and needed some change of scenery. I'd made it about half way to Hot Springs when I decided to stop and make a phone call about a piece of gear that needed to be replaced.

While I was on hold, I began walking my bike out of boredom. After I walked about thirty yards from where I had started the phone call, a car came speeding around into sight. It looked like they were going too fast to make the upcoming curve safely, and sure enough they slid off of the road right where I was standing.

They didn't wreck but their back end whipped across the grass right where I was standing before I started to walk. If I hadn't walked those few feet I would've been smashed! After I finished my phone call I stood there thinking about how close I had just come to being hit, shrugged it off, and made my way for Hot Springs.

Hot Springs was really nice compared to Little Rock. Less people meant less stress for me. It's wild how just a few miles can make you feel like you're entering another country. Besides the obvious changes, the first thing I noticed was the Hot Springs Mountain Tower. I didn't know what the tower was about but I knew I wanted to get up there for a good view and some fresh air.

As I was making my way through town, I began to notice a lot of Christmas decorations. I hadn't really been keeping up with my days but it made sense. Christmas has always been my favorite holiday and it wouldn't be too long from now. I wondered where and how I'd spend it as I made my way up the mountain.

When I got to the top I felt like the ride up was totally worth it. I had to skip out on the tower, though. I'm not even sure what the tower is about but you had to pay to ride it to the top. I just sat across from it inside of this concrete gazebo.

From Hot Springs, I decided that I would drop down

to highway 70 and see how far west I could take that before I got bored of it. I had some new gear being sent to the post office in De Queen, anyways. I was kind of locked into a route for now. Oh, and in case you are were wondering how to get mail while traveling, you simply have the package sent to a post office as general delivery. A lot of people often wondered how I got mail so I thought I'd throw that in here.

Before making my way down to De Queen I needed to see a doctor because I was having some trouble sleeping. I found a doctor's office in Glenwood but they couldn't see me until the next day.

I was already there so I decided to sleep behind it. So much for sleep, though. That was the whole reason I was there. The nurse understood my situation and gave me something to help me sleep.

I hadn't slept well in a while and it was really starting to take its toll on me. You'd think cycling all day would wear you out enough, but maybe I was a bit manic. Who knows? I camped between Glenwood and Daisy that night and I was able to finally get some sleep!

The next day, on my way to Daisy, I stopped at a church to have breakfast. They had a picnic table so it seemed like the perfect place to take a quick break. While I was eating, I noticed a truck that kept passing by and the driver was eyeballing me down. It wasn't long after that a police officer arrived to ask me what I was doing. What did it look like I was doing? Some people act like they've never seen a traveler before. I explained what I was doing and they still said that I had to leave. That was a strange church anyways. Who puts a basketball goal and volleyball net up in their cemetery?

When I made it to Daisy I decided to swing in and check out the lake at Crawford Park. It was really peaceful here. I walked along the lake and took it all in. I needed that after being forced to leave a church for eating breakfast. I didn't let that get me down, though.

The lake was a great place to just chill out. Then I made my way to Dierks where I ran into a man at a gas station. I told him what I was doing and he said that I was the bravest man he'd ever met; that I was living his dream, and if he wasn't ninety years old he would have joined me. It sure was nice to hear that!

It was getting dark as I was leaving Daisy but I wanted to make it into De Queen so I would be able to pick up my things from the post office and be on my way. Somewhere along the way I realized that I had dropped my gloves. I must have backtracked ten miles before giving up. No glove, no love. I turned back around and did some night riding. I made it into De Queen around 10:00 pm and camped out behind a Polaris store.

3

I carried my new supplies over to a bench to pack them into my saddle bags. I would have been there only a few minutes before packing up to leave but this man walked over to me from his office. His said his name was Randell and I talked to him about how I was cycling across America for mental health awareness. He reached into his pocket to hand me some candies and hot cocoa mix.

I don't recommend taking candy from strangers, kids, but you learn how to pass judgment; and he seemed like a good guy. After he went back into his office I began putting on my new tires. I spent a good portion of my money on some new Schwalbe Marathon Plus tires, but I was sick of getting so many flats. Less flats would mean more miles. Hopefully these would turn out to be a good investment.

Randell came back outside as I was getting on my bike to leave. He said he felt bad for just giving me candy and handed me seventy dollars! I laughed and thanked him before heading on my way. He really was a nice guy! Seventy dollars will go a long way out here! So long as you don't run into any serious issues with your gear anyway.

I crossed on over into Oklahoma and camped in the

woods behind a bar outside of Broken Bow. The bar was fairly busy that night but luckily no one came wandering over near my tent. I heard a few feral hogs come close, though. Luckily, they didn't stick around very long. The boars out here can get massive. They're usually easy to scare off but they could rip you to shreds if they wanted to.

The next morning, I made way into Broken Bow and stopped at a McDonald's to eat breakfast and charge my phone. I had a SunTactics solar panel but it was useless due to the heavy overcast. All I needed was enough charge so I could look at my map and decide on what route I wanted to take. An atlas would have come in handy during times like these; especially in Oklahoma, where you'd be lucky to get any cellular service!

While I was waiting for my phone to charge the manager came over and said I had to leave because I was a tripping hazard. I looked around and I couldn't disagree with her. Everyone that was coming into the restaurant was looking at me instead of where they were going. People here must not be used to travelers. Either that or I must have been looking rather haggard at this point! I was a little irritated but I will admit that I laughed on the inside. That was, after all, the first place that I'd ever been kicked out of; but it wouldn't be the last.

A local here by the name of Scott had been following my blog and he was outraged about how I had been treated there. He was at work at the time but he sent a friend out to find me. My phone was dead at this point so they had no way to contact me. His friend found me just as I was getting ready to leave Walmart. He said he had been looking all over for me.

I was just as glad as he was that he found me because he offered me forty dollars! The money I spent on those tires had been restored and my financial worries weren't in question anymore. I decided to use a few bucks to get a new machete, some food to store in my saddle bags, and a pair of Heritage Extreme Winter Gloves.

As I was leaving Broken Bow I realized that it was Christmas Eve. I wanted to make sure I found a place to camp where I could have a fire. A few miles from Hugo and I found the perfect spot. I found a small pine tree and decided to decorate it with my chain lock and some carabiners. Underneath my Christmas tree I laid two beers, the hot chocolate Randell had given me, and the machete that I had just bought. It was beginning to look a lot like Christmas!

I put my tent up and got everything ready to build a nice fire. Once I had my fire going I decided to heat me up a can of chicken Alfredo. It was much better than eating it frozen and it paired nicely with my two beers. The moon was high and full so I made the fire just large enough to last me through my meal. The moon would provide plenty of light if I needed it. I crawled into my tent and fell asleep to the coyotes singing again.

I woke to a lovely, frigid Christmas morning and decided to build another fire. It wasn't the cold that made me want to build a fire, though. I just wanted to enjoy the hot cocoa that was still lying beneath my tree! I got packed up soon after I finished my cocoa and headed into town. I was in no rush, though. I had a care package coming from a lady named Lori, but I couldn't get it until tomorrow.

I had a pretty good Christmas in Hugo. On my way into town a man stopped to give me a banana, the HiWay Inn Hotel let me take a shower, one lady gave me a box with sausage, cheese, and crackers, and another lady gave me twenty dollars! I felt a lot of peace and love from all of these strangers. I ended my day early at a park that I found while checking out the town. Since it was Christmas, there weren't too many people out. I had the whole park to myself and it was so relaxing. I couldn't have asked for a better Christmas!

The next day, as I was making my way to the post office, I decided to toss my antidepressant medication into the trash. I had been taking them for a few years but slowly weaned myself off of them. I hadn't felt depressed in a while and I was certain that this was contributed to my lifestyle change. Exercise, being outdoors, keeping it simple and humble; these were the things I believed to be making me happy. I felt empowered when I finally tossed the last of my medication.

I waited outside of the post office until they opened so I could pick up my care package. This was the first time someone sent me care package so I was pretty excited. Inside of the package was several granola bars, trail mix, batteries for my headlamp, a couple of cookies, a toothbrush and toothpaste, and a letter with words of encouragement. Lori had a traumatic brain injury and appreciated me spreading awareness for mental health. After loading up all the goodies she had sent I was on my way to Texas!

By the time I reached Paris, TX it had been raining for a while. I had dawned my rain gear but it gets annoying after riding in it for several hours. I decided to sit outside of the Budget Inn to let the worse of it pass. Once it calmed down a little I pushed on for Bonham, but I wouldn't make it all the way before needing to find a spot to camp.

It was already cold and there was a cold front moving in behind this storm. I was ready for the temperatures to drop. I felt like I thrived in it and people just never seemed to understand that about me. At least when it's cold you can layer up. When it's hot you can only remove so much before it becomes indecent. This night outside of Bonham I would get my wish, though.

I made my way down to Dallas, Texas from here. My friend, Robbie, from Tennessee had moved here a few years ago. I hadn't seen him or his family in a while so I figured this would be a great opportunity. I stayed with them for two days and it was nice to catch up with them. Some home cooked meals, a couch to sleep on, a nice warm shower, and my clothes got a good wash. The little break here was great for my body and soul. Getting back on the road after some rejuvenation felt great!

I made my way to Throckmorton from here but before I made it there I was stopped on the side of the road by an older man. He stepped out of his car and talked to me about my travels for a few minutes. Then he popped the strangest question, "What's your favorite pie?" I felt a little confused by this question but I replied, "Hmm.. Probably pecan. Why?" He walked back to his car and opened his trunk. He told me to come over to him, so I did. He pulled out a pecan pie and handed it to me! I looked into the drunk and there weren't any other pies so I was really shocked! He told me to enjoy it and have a safe trip.

I posted on my blog what had just happened and it turned out there were several people in the area who were following me. They all knew of this man. They said that he rode around and gave homeless people pies. I thought that was really cool but I was still confused as to how he had exactly what I said I liked, nothing more and nothing less. I wondered what would have happened if I said any other type of pie! By the time I had made it into Throckmorton it was just getting dark and I made my way behind another church.

I posted a picture of where I was camping for the night and just a few minutes later a lady contacted me. She offered to bring me a hot meal for the night. She showed up with a hot meal and her two kids, and asked if it would be okay for them to get me a motel room. I took the offer because nothing out here beats a warm bed and shower! Man, was I glad I ran into them! I had a bivy being delivered here the next day to swap it out for my tent, too. So, it was perfect timing!

It didn't take long for me to regret swapping out my tent for that bivy, though. That next night I got caught up in a storm and the bivy really let me down. Everything was soaking wet by the next morning and the temperatures were about to drop below freezing. I was hoping that everything would dry that next day but when I made it into Haskell I realized that everything was still soaking wet. I knew I was in trouble because it was supposed to get down into the teens that night. I didn't know what else to do besides hunker down and hope I made it through.

I found a motel on my map and decided that I would go over and ask if they had a dryer that I could use. When I got there, they refused to let me use their dryer until the man, Ed, came out and talked to me. He thought his wife, Angie, was crazy for refusing to let me use their dryer. I got to dry everything and they even offered me a free room for the night. Such a blessing!

As I was settling down in my room, Ed came over and told me to come to the front for breakfast in the morning. They didn't have continental breakfasts here. They lived at the motel, though, so they were basically offering me into their home. Over breakfast, they told me that they initially turned me down because they have been courteous to several travelers that turned around to make a mess of things; and their boss wasn't too happy with their decisions. They turned out to be really nice people after all and we still keep in touch.

Just a few more days now and I'll be in Roswell, New Mexico. I've always been intrigued by Roswell's history of the UFO crash, so this was a definite stop for me. When I got into town I was hunted down by a newspaper reporter. We met up and he offered me to come to his house. There wasn't any room in his car for me and my gear but that was fine with me. He gave me his address and I met up with him to do my first interview. I ended up camping in his backyard for two days before the interview was finished but he made sure I was well fed!

After I left the reporter's house I had to go see a dermatologist for a sore on my nose and back that wouldn't go away. The spots had been there since the sunburn I got back in Florida, so I had good reason to be worried. They turned out to be benign, thankfully!

After I left the dermatologist the receptionist there gave me a call and offered me a stay at her house. I ended up staying with her for two days and we had a lot of fun. It was nice to have some casual company instead of the usual traveling conversations. As much as I enjoyed our time together, I had to be on my way.

After I left her house I stopped by a gas station to fill up on water before heading out. I was sitting outside next to the newspaper stand when I noticed that I was on the front page. Man, that was a strange feeling! I decided to grab on of the papers and read the article for myself. The reporter had worded things up to his liking, but they weren't exactly right. I was a little upset but I learned firsthand that reporters will twist your story to make it more exciting.

While I was sitting there reading the article I was offered two free nights at a hotel so I could do a radio interview. Word was really starting to spread now and I had my chance to give everyone my story, instead of the way the reporter had it in the paper. I went to drop my things off at the hotel and then headed downtown to check out all of the cool alien museums. Since the museums knew who I was, I got to see everything for free. Too cool!

The next day I got to go down to the radio station to be interviewed on three different stations. I was finally able to get the word out about how exercise plays an important role on mental health awareness. It felt a little invasive telling everyone that I struggled with post-traumatic stress disorder and bipolar disorder. It shouldn't be that big of a deal but there is a lot of stigma against mental disorders. However, I was here to talk about the difference all of this exercise has had on me.

After I left the radio station, and getting to hang out with all of the nice broadcasters, I ran into people who had just heard me on the radio. Four men who also had PTSD stopped to talk to me about it and said that I was doing a great thing out there. That helped to put a little more pep in my step! The number of followers on my blog began to climb quite rapidly, too!

One more night in the hotel and I'd be on my way out of here. That night I was contacted by the first reporter. He said his friend owned an Italian restaurant in town called Carmine's and wanted me to swing by for a free lunch. I'm glad I did! Before I left Roswell, I made sure to come back for one more plate. It was too good to pass up on seconds, even though I had to pay for the second round. That's how they get you!

A few miles out of Roswell and I ran into more mountains. It had been flat for so long and the land was definitely starting to take change. The trees had become shrubs and the grass was replaced by rocks and dirt. And, by the time I had reached Hondo Valley, it had even begun to snow!

I received several winter storm advisories so I knew it was going to get bad pretty soon. As the snow began to pile up I had made my way into San Patricio. Coming into town I noticed a sign on the side of the road that read " STATE COP AHEAD WITH A BAD ATTITUDE, PMS, AND A GUN". I got a pretty good laugh out of that. I never saw a cop out that way but maybe it was for the best.

It appeared as though the whole town was shut down. It was probably because of the snow and no one wanted to be out in it. There were a lot of historical sites here, though. I made sure to check out as many as I could. Most of them had to do with Lincoln's Army's settlement during the 1850s. Some of the forts looked as though they could still be put to use; you might want to patch up some of the bullet holes, though!

When I made it into Capitan the snow had really began to stack up. I had been focused on all of the beauty surrounding me that I had completely neglected to put my balaclava on. The high altitude, mixed with the frigid air, had set me up for a sore throat and a frost covered beard. Luckily, though, when I made it into town, I ran into a woman named Trish. She offered to purchase me a warm meal from the gas station. It really hit the spot and since it was getting late, a warm meal came just in time before I crawled into my tent.

I wasn't sure where to set up camp here in Capitan, but I wanted to stay close to town so I could grab some coffee in the morning. I came across an RV camp and asked the owners if I could camp out back. They gave me the okay. There was about eight inches of snow on the ground and there was more on the way. When I woke up there was about a foot of snow on the ground now. The snow had accumulated on my tent and when I stepped out it looked like someone had built an igloo.

I made my way over to the gas station for my morning coffee when I ran into a real mountain man. He was legitimate alright. His name was Ray and we talked for about an hour. He said he used to live in Alaska and moved down here a few years ago. He wasn't a mountain man anymore but he still had it in him.

He talked about different types of shelters, traps, weapons, anything you could imagine he had an answer for it. Unfortunately, he moved down here for cancer treatment and turned to alcohol. I wonder if he's still around? He was a really cool dude. An old man who had lived most of his life in the wild. Hats off to this man. I'd best be on my way.

Making my way back into the mountains out of Capitan was quite difficult. I had a good distance between where I was and Carrizozo. The mountains were covered in ice so it took me longer than it normally would. I didn't have snow tires or any zip ties to help keep any traction. I tried my hardest to keep an eye out for dry spots so I could keep on the move. Going down an ice-covered mountain at 45 mph was pretty intense. I finally made it into town, though, and I was offered a free motel room at the Rainbow Inn. Thanks, Scott!

The ride to Kiritimati was pretty much the same as it had been since Capitan. The snow and ice was finally starting to disappear as I lowered in elevation. I was able to put down some pretty good distance today. I camped just outside of The Valley of The Fire. I couldn't wait to check out this historic site tomorrow! US 380 between Carrizozo and San Antonio was subject to closure due to missile firing. They gave a number to keep drivers updated, but since I was on a bike, I really just wanted to get through there!

After I checked out The Valley of The Fire, I began climbing some more mountains. I turned around to look at how much ground I had covered and saw the mountains I had just came from. I was frozen by how beautiful they looked from a different perspective. I actually couldn't believe that I had just made it through all of those mountains in just a couple of days. I turned to look back at them several times. It was the perfect spot to just sit in awe at the beauty all around me. Snow covered mountains as far as I could see.

I had fifty more miles to San Antonio from the top of the mountain I was standing on. Most of it was coasting downhill followed by one more mountain. Then things would start to flatten out. I was loving the mountains but my body was getting tired from the uphill battles and lack of oxygen in the higher altitudes.

I made it into Socorro before dark. A few people had heard of me passing through and offered to take me out to dinner. I ended meeting five or six of them that loaded my bike into their truck and took me to one of their favorite restaurants. I can only remember a few of the people but I'm sure they all remember me! Barbie, Kris, Marty, and Jonah. Yeah, they were awesome company! I ended up staying the night at their house where we played beer pong and acted like normal people our age. It was nice to have some company that wasn't all about me!

It wasn't time for me to leave yet, though. I had a couple of other people wanting to meet me in Socorro; Amy and Marcus. We sat around for a while and had some good talks. Mostly good, anyways. Marcus was telling me about all of the mountain lion sightings in the area.

That made me a little nervous but I didn't really care too much about wild animals anymore. Her kids were playing and trying to figure out why a stranger was in their house! Amy just wanted me to stop by so she could make me a BLT. I wasn't hungry at the time so I put it into my saddle bags.

Shortly after I left Amy's house a motorist pulled over. An older man stepped out of his car and walked up to me. I noticed he was holding a camera so I thought "Okay. Here we go. I got another reporter I bet." Sure enough! He worked for the Socorro paper and wanted to do an interview. He snagged a picture of me and said he needed to run back into town to grab his tape recorder. I told him to go ahead but I might be a few more miles.

When the reporter finally caught back up with me I was already in Magdalena. I must have been manic at the time because that was a pretty good stretch through a lot of mountains. Having bipolar disorder has its perks sometimes. Good thing I used up a lot of my energy, though, or I may have gone off talking about who knows what. We sat outside of the fire station and had our interview. Once he thought he had gathered enough information we parted ways. I still had maybe an hour left of daylight so I stopped by a local store here to fill up on water and continued on.

I found a great spot to camp for the night outside of Magdalena. I was just off of the road but behind a hill. I liked to keep out of sight whenever I could. I had a wonderful view to sit and enjoy my sandwich Amy had given me. I decided to go ahead and use this medicinal plant that I had been hanging onto. It would help me get some sleep since my mind had been racing all day. Good thing I didn't venture far from my tent. I was sitting maybe fifty feet away and barely made it back. That sure was some potent stuff! I should be well rested for tomorrow.

The next morning, I packed up and made my way for Datil. I didn't know the VLA (Very Large Array) was located between Datil and Socorro. When I saw the sign I just had to make my way over to it. It was a bit out of the way but I wanted a closer look. I'm guessing the road to it was about five miles but totally worth checking out since I was already there.

The VLA has a visitor center so I was hoping to get a tour of the place, but they weren't working that day. It was still worth stopping by to grab a picture and say that I've been there!

After I had made my way back onto the highway I ran into a couple from Germany who were cycling across the United States as well. They were hoping to go check out the VLA as well but I saved them the extra miles. They were curious as to why I was heading west instead of east. The head winds make cycling west pretty difficult but I explained to them that I was heading for Alaska.

There were days that were so windy that, even when traveling down the side of a mountain, I would have to dismount. It's no fun having to walk your bike down a mountain when you just finished struggling to reach the top!

I made it into Datil just in time for lunch. I pulled over at the store to grab a bite to eat. They had stopped making lunch for the winter. I asked the man how far it was until I could find a restaurant and he laughed. "You're not going to find anything for quite a way. All of the restaurants are shut down for the winter." Well, I guess I'd best be on my way then! Maybe Pie Town would have something.

I made it about ten miles from Pie Town before it got dark. I found a place to sleep just off of the side of the highway again. It didn't really matter out here. I hadn't seen any traffic for hours. It looked like the people that I met back at the VLA may have camped here. If it was good enough for them then it was good enough for me.

It was January 26th now and up here in the mountains it was dropping down into the single digits. I remember waking up at some point because the moon was so bright and it sounded like all of the animals around me were performing some kind of ritual; a very loud one at that. I was shivering and decided to get out and exercise to warm my body up. I actually had to do this a lot. The cooler days made it easier to travel but the nights took a bit of work.

The next morning, I finally crossed the Continental Divide at an elevation of 7,796 feet. I knew I wasn't far from Pie Town now. I've heard of a lot of hikers stopping here. It isn't called Pie Town for nothing! I was hoping to get a slice but when I got there everything was shut down. Go figure. The gas station was still open, though. I made my way over to grab a cup of coffee and a small snack. I needed some fuel!

Before leaving Pie Town I made my way over to a park where I could see a porta potty. That coffee was making its way through and I needed to restock on toilet paper. After I used the restroom I decided to check out the dumpsters for anything I could use. That's when I realized that I was in bear country. I hadn't seen one in a while but they were here. The proof was in the paw print. I'll be out of their territory by tonight, though. Not that I had anything for them to be interested in anyways. I was out here scavenging just like the rest of them.

By the end of the day, just as the sun was going down, I was on top of my last big mountain. I could see Arizona in the distance. I wasn't close enough to see a sign or anything, but I knew I was getting close. I was pretty excited to know I'd be crossing into another state come morning. My last night in New Mexico I ended up pitching my tent right next to someone's old sleeping pad. We travelers must start thinking alike after a few months.

I was making my way for my Arizona sign when I decided to take a break at rest stop. A family pulled over and handed me a can of ravioli and some crackers. Man, I really needed that! I had a few bucks on me so I offered to pay them for the food. They refused to take it, though. Their kindness gave me a full belly and the motivation I needed to get back on the road.

After a several hours of pedaling through some canyons I finally made it to Arizona! There were two state troopers parked next to the state sign. They came over to ask where I was heading and offered to take my picture. I was still pretty hungry and asked them how far I was from the next restaurant. They said I could find one coming up in Springerville.

I can't remember the name of the restaurant but it was in Springerville, AZ. It felt good to be in a town where things were actually open. I would spend a few minutes looking over the menu, only to feel hungrier and hungrier. I didn't have enough money to buy a burger. Everything was so expensive here. I guess that's what to expect from a small town, though. I offered to trade them one of my external batteries for a meal and they accepted it. I didn't mind! It had been a few days since I had a large meal. This should last me a while.

It wasn't long after I left Springerville when I found myself in Eagar. I decided to take some time here to explore. I'm not sure why I chose to stick around Eagar all day but I'm glad I did. After taking some side roads, I came across a skate park. I grew up skateboarding and thought about how cool it'd be if I had a board with me. It had been a while since, though. I'd probably end up with some broken ankles. It was probably best that I didn't see a board lying around!

After I left the skate park I spotted a fire station. I remembered reading somewhere how hikers would stop at fire houses to get a shower so I decided to stop by and ask. When I walked in, there was a lady inside cleaning up the place. I asked her if they had a shower I could use and she asked, "are you one of those hiker guys?" Close enough! It became obvious that she has seen a few come through for a shower. She showed me to the wash house and I was able to get a shower. I went ahead and got some laundry done, too. I felt like a new man! Clean enough to go grab a bite to eat at Arby's.

I ordered some curly fries at the Arby's in Eagar when I noticed that they weren't curly. I jokingly posted about it on my blog and Arby's offered me a free meal. Seriously? A free meal because I said the fries weren't curly? I'll take that! But don't take advantage of Arby's. I'm sure they work hard to curl their fries!

Now that I was full and had clean clothes hanging all over my bike, it was time to find a place to camp. I noticed a water tower on top of a hill and decided to head on up to see what it was like. It turned out to be a cemetery but I didn't see why anyone would come up here. I'd sleep here tonight and be able to come back down in the morning to get a cup of coffee before making my way into St. Johns. A couple of teenagers came up to hang out at the graveyard but when they saw me and my tent they decided to leave.

When I woke up the next morning there were a couple of trucks that had pulled into the cemetery. I'm not sure what they were doing but I think they were eating breakfast. Man, this must be a hot spot for local gatherings! I felt a bit awkward crawling out of a tent with these men watching me. Just add to the fact that this all took place in a cemetery. Who camps in a cemetery? Who eats breakfast in a cemetery? I know they had to be curious. Why didn't they ask what I was doing? Oh, well, time to be heading out. I just have to be weird sometimes.

As I was making my way for St. Johns I passed through Lyman Lake State Park. It was quite the scenery out here. I had to stop and take a walk around one of the creeks that I had seen. I was looking for animal tracks mostly. I wanted to see what other visitors had made their way to this stream. Just a few coyotes. I'd better be getting along, though. There was a storm was moving in. I didn't have service to check the weather but I could just tell. The air pressure felt like it was dropping and I still had a pretty good way to go, and no idea what St Johns would have in store for me; if anything at all.

It began to rain as I came into St Johns. My first impression was that this was a ghost town. It looked like a couple of deserted junkyards. I eventually made my way into town, though, and it wasn't as deserted as I thought. It was pretty late by the time I got there so I decided to find a place to camp here for the night. I found a church with a large building in the back. There were several picnic tables but nothing else. There was a bad storm heading this way. I'd sleep under the building for added shelter. As you may remember from earlier in my travels, I'm not a very big fan of lightning.

The next day it was still raining but I decided to ride through it. I was heading for Petrified Forest and I was pretty excited about it. Rain wasn't going to slow me down! I didn't make to the welcome center until dark, though. I found a wooden tepee next to the entrance and decided to stay inside for the night. There was another storm heading my way. I probably would have been better off just staying in my tent, but it added some change to my routine. I was asleep in the tepee for a few hours before the storm had hit.

I was just sleeping on the ground when I was awakened by the feeling of water. The ground was dry when I fell asleep but it had all turned into mud. My sleeping pad and sleeping bag were soaked. Probably not my best choice! I immediately got up and grabbed a few boards that were lying up against the inside walls. I used them to make a quick little bench to sleep on. The floor may be leaking but the roof was fine. The storm got pretty bad that night. It definitely made things interesting!

The next morning, even though I was cold, wet, and

covered in mud, I was excited to get to go through the Petrified Forest. As I made my way to the entrance gate the chain on my bike broke. Man, that was a real bummer. I was a long way from anywhere to get a new chain, nor did I have any chain links with me. I shrugged it off. There wasn't really anything I could do. I decided to go ahead and walk my bike through the national forest.

I quickly realized that I had to pay a fee in order to go in. Man, I just didn't have enough cash on me for that. Oh, well. I decided to turn back to the highway and continue north. I needed to use the restroom first, though. So, I went into the welcome center. I used the restroom there yesterday so I knew they had one. When I walked in I asked if I could use their restroom. There was a different lady working than the day before.

She told me they didn't have one. I told her I used it yesterday, that it was right back there. She went on to say that I couldn't use it because I was dirty. They didn't want me in there doing laundry and cleaning up. I said "Ma'am, I'm not sure what difference it would make if I decided to clean up in there, but I assure you that I just have to pee. I won't make a mess." She replied, "I'm sorry but you can't come in here like that. We don't want you in there brushing your teeth." Yes, that was her exact quote!

Okay, so now I'm soaking wet, covered in mud, cold, I got refused to use the bathroom, and I have to push my bike for who knows how long. I'll admit that I retaliated by pissing on the side of their building, though. I shouldn't have done that but that lady was a total bitch. If I would have needed to poop they really would have hated me!

It was only a twenty mile walk until I made it into my next town of Holbrook. It took me all day to get there but I loved the change of pace. It was dark when I got there so I didn't want to go into the city limits. I ended up camping behind the welcome sign. Tomorrow I would see if I could find a chain for my bike.

The next morning, an older couple saw me pushing my

bike and decided to stop and ask if I needed a lift. I declined their offer but asked if they knew of anywhere that I could pick up a chain. "You might have some luck at Walt's Hardware. We can give you a ride there and take you out to eat if you're interested", the man said. I took them up on that!

I was able to find a chain. I didn't know if it would fit or not, though. The couple said they were going to go pick up some lunch and could meet me at the dog park. It was right down the road and it would give me some time to try and put my new chain on. The chain fit somewhat but it skipped a lot. Looks like I'll be limping my way down the interstate until I made it to Flagstaff. At least I had some good conversation and lunch with the couple that stopped to help. Nice folks!

The next thirty miles into Winslow weren't too bad. My chain was working well enough to keep me going downhill. I finally made it to the truck stop just after dark. I couldn't see much of my surroundings but I knew that if I couldn't see it then no one else could either. I stood at the entrance to Love's for a few minutes, watching the headlights shoot off into the desert. After a few minutes of that I would know where I could camp. No one would see me here and I'd be able to grab my cup of coffee in the morning.

It was a foggy morning and I didn't feel like it would be very wise to push my bike down the interstate. I sat next to the on-ramp for about an hour with my thumb out. No one stopped, though. By this time the fog had lifted and I felt okay with getting back to it. I would have hated taking a ride anyways.

I made my way into Meteor City before dark. I wanted to check out the crater but it was pretty far out of the way and would cost money to see it. I figured I'd better just be on my way into Flagstaff. I had to stop and get a picture with this large dream catcher, though. I think it was made of PVC pipe but I could be wrong. It was large enough to stand in with my face poking through the center. I had to get a picture of that! People who were following my blog always thought someone was with me because of my pictures but I was indeed alone. Cameras have timers on them these days!

It wasn't long after I left Meteor City that I was able to see Mt. Humphrey's Peak. It was good to have a landmark to lead me into Flagstaff but judging from the size of the mountain I probably still had about fifty miles to go. That's an easy two-day hike when you're pushing all of your gear that's strapped to a bike.

I walked through the dark for a while before I stopped. I must have made it pretty far because I made it into Flagstaff around lunch time the next day. I sure did choose an interesting place to camp for the night between cities, though. Since I was still on the interstate there weren't too many places to go.

I found a concrete tunnel underneath the road and decided it would do. My options were limited. At least here I wouldn't have to unload my bike and throw everything over a fence. As soon as I got off of the interstate and made it into Flagstaff, I was pulled over by a police officer. He said it was because I was riding on the wrong side of the road but if that was the case then I think he could have gone without all of the questioning.

As I made my way into Flagstaff, I realized that it was bike friendly community. There were cyclists everywhere! So, maybe the police officer was justified in pulling me over. When there is a lot of anything going on in a particular place you can bet they will have strict laws on it. Bikes are no exception to this.

I made my way down to the nearest bike shop and had them slap a new chain on there for me. Everyone was kind of eye balling me down because I had so much gear. It must have been obvious that I wasn't from around here.

When I asked the shop owners about the chain they were like, "Yeah. We can do that. Just bring it up here when you get all of that gear off." I was so used to doing this that it took me about thirty seconds to have my bike stripped down to nothing. I had someone try to go around me in line until they realized that I was able to do this before the line even moved. I thought that was funny.

After I got my bike fixed up and ready to go I was ready to find me some food! I think I had about $200 saved up from all of the people helping me out along the way, so I decided to swing by a Mexican restaurant and get me a taco with a Corona. That sounded good to me!

I knew I was going to be in Flagstaff for a few days because I needed to order a new sleeping bag. The one that I was using had a busted zipper on it. Not really a big deal but it was still under warranty and I figured I might as well use it.

That night I ended up running into a guy name Skip. He had been following my page for a while and saw that I was in town. He met up with me and asked if I would like for him to get me a motel room. Heck yeah, I would!

After he left me to my room I was pretty quick to jump in the shower. Man, that's the best thing about getting a motel room right there. At this point being inside feels strange to me but it's nice to be able to let your guard down so you can get some deep sleep, too. Even if I did sleep on the floor in my sleeping bag.

I'm used to just running around doing whatever so I got bored pretty quick. I decided to make a dating profile and see if I'd have any luck with the ladies. Sure enough! I should have done this a long time ago. This girl came and hung out with me for a few hours. That was fun!

The next morning, I decided to just ride around and check out the neighborhood. I was in a good mood and telling everyone good morning but no one would say it back. Looking back at it I probably just looked crazy. Hardly anyone is happy with their lives anymore. That's the difference that doing what you enjoy will make.

I ran into this one guy name Gabriel, though. He was kind of like me. A traveler on a bike. He had been staying in Flagstaff for a few months with a few other cyclists. They were like a hippie family but almost like Amish? I'm not really sure what their deal was but they were all nice and kept everything simple.

Gabriel took me to check out some good camping spots that he would recommend if I was going to be sticking around for a few days. We went to the northwest side of the city, out past the Lowell Observatory, and it was awesome out there!

I think this has to be one of my favorite places that I visited. You could go into town and when it got to be too much you could just wander off into the woods. It seemed like most of the people preferred staying in the city for whatever reason, and I definitely didn't mind. It was still pretty early but Gabriel was ready to head back to his house. I decided to stick around out here while I was waiting for Jody to make his way up from Phoenix.

It was starting to get dark and Jody would be here soon so I made my way back into town. We decided to meet up at Pizza Hut where we would be celebrating his birthday. I actually didn't know it was his birthday until way later. This is what he chose to do for his birthday, though. He wanted to hang out with the guy who was traveling across the United States.

I got there about thirty minutes before he did so I went ahead and picked us out a table. I decided to go ahead and get me a beer while I waited. I was pretty excited to meet him too. He had sent me several care packages along the way and seemed like a really cool guy.

There was no mistaking him when he walked through the door. Big ole biker dude with some wild hair and a bushy beard. Big ole grin on his face too! You could just tell he was a good guy from the way he presented himself. I knew I was in good company.

He brought his wife and grandchildren along with him. I think I may have seemed a little scary to them at first. Like "Why did you want to come hang out with this homeless guy for your birthday." Ha! But they all ended up liking me before the night was over. I'm pretty good with kids, I think. I love the spirit they have inside of them. That was basically the spirit I was running on at this point. I was just a grown-up version.

We had us a few beers and a couple of pizzas, and mostly talked about all that I had been through up to this point. Jody said he'd always wanted to do something like what I'm doing and admired me for actually taking some initiative.

Maybe that's what intrigued him about me the most. The fact that he's had the idea to do it but never did. What was it that sat us apart. What drove me into doing something that he thought was only a fantasy?

It made me feel thankful that I took advantage of my situation and went for it. That's really the only thing that sets me apart from anyone else who wants to do something like this. Everything I had was just taken from me. I had nothing tying me down.

We were getting up to leave and it was bittersweet. I could really get used to hanging out with this guy but he had to get back home and I had my journey to continue.

We went out to the parking lot, stumbling around a little bit from all the beers we just had, and got a group picture. Then he walked over to his truck and pulled out a bag full of food. I had scored another care package!

There was way too much for me to carry but I asked if I could share some with me new friend Gabriel and he gave me the okay. I knew Gabriel was around here somewhere dumpster diving so I couldn't wait to find him and share the goods. Thanks, Jody! Happy birthday!

I didn't have much energy after I parted ways with Jody, so I just walked down the street until I found dark spot to get some sleep. I just threw my sleeping pad on the ground beside a tree and that was the end of my night.

The next morning, I made my way over to the UPS store so I could pick up my new sleeping bag and send the old one off. I ended up running into Gabriel while I was there and gave him a few handfuls of food from the bag Jody had given me the night before.

He asked if I'd like to come over and have dinner with this family later and I said I would love to. He told me they were a bit skeptical of strangers, though. He would have to check with them and make sure it was okay. So, I gave him my number and took the rest of my day to wander off into the woods that he had introduced me to.

He called me later in the afternoon and told me to meet him back at the UPS store and then I could follow him to their house. So, I hurried back down into town and there he was.

He warned me that the people he lives with are a little strange. Not in a scary way but the way they live is just different outside of the norm. Did he know who he was talking to? Obviously not. Let's go meet these people you call strange!

They were definitely different, indeed. I mentioned that earlier but I'll go into more details now that we're all caught up. They were, like I said before, an Amish-like group of people. Something between Amish, hippies, and nomads. I don't mean that in a bad way, though. I found them to be very unique and interesting. The way they lived was fascinating.

They were a small grouped family all coming from different walks of life. I would say there were about fifteen of them. The women wore dresses and the men wore aprons. Some of them were married and had kids. But they all lived together.

As for now, they had a house here in Flagstaff but said they would be on the move again soon. They were basically running an underground bike shop from their house and the town was wanting them to stop their business.

They only traveled by bikes. Even the kids. The cycled all over with the adults and were home schooled. You might wonder how the kids were doing as far as their learning goes given the circumstance. They were actually smarter than most public-school kids I had met.

One of the younger boys was around six years old and had designed his own motor for his bike that ran off of water. He had a motor connected to his bike that created electricity which separated the hydrogen from the oxygen.

I'm not here to give away exactly what I saw but I was thoroughly impressed. And, like me, he wanted to run off to Alaska and live in the wild, so he was pretty envious to know that's where I was headed.

Dinner was ready and they had some strict rules regarding how they ate. I didn't want to be disrespectful or interrupt how they normally did things. Gabriel told me to just follow along, but basically to just let the women and children get their food first. The men would then get whatever was left from oldest to youngest and eat facing away from the women. It was a little strange to me but I enjoyed it.

After dinner, we sat around and talked for a while and then at some point someone mentioned bringing out a guitar. I used to play guitar religiously back in the day so I was pretty excited. It had been a while since I had the joy of playing.

4

One of the guys put the guitar down and I asked if they'd mind if I played it for a bit. "Sure! Go ahead!" And then everyone joined around to watch me play. I was a little nervous since it had been so long. Thankfully, it all came back to me, and I was playing songs that everyone knew. We were singing and having a good time. I felt like they had accepted me which was pretty amazing since they seemed to be a culture of all their own.

As the day was coming to an end they said that I could camp in their back yard if I wanted and then join them for breakfast in the morning. Sounded like a good idea to me! The next morning, the oldest man at Gabriel's came out to see if I was awake. They sure do get up early around here. It was still dark out. My kind of people!

We went back into the house and everyone was gone except for the old man and one of the younger women. She was the one cooking breakfast. I'm not sure where everyone else had gone off too. I wondered if she was just making breakfast for me. I'd feel kind of bad if that were the case but I didn't ask. I just accepted their kindness.

I sat and ate with the lady. We had sausage, bagels, eggs, and a spoon of almond butter. That was the first time that I had tried almond butter. Everywhere I had seen it was really expensive so I never bothered with it; but it was amazing!

I noted how I'd never tried it before and asked about the jar it was in. It was just a plain mason jar. She said that they make it themselves because it's really good but too expensive to buy from the store. Made sense to me! She even gave me a little jar to carry with me on the road. Man, that was some good stuff and didn't last me very long! Now I'm always going to be on the hunt for it.

After we got through eating I went ahead and gathered my things to get out of there. I really enjoyed their company and didn't want to overstay my welcome. Remember my description of these people. If you see them you will know exactly who they are!

Before I left Flagstaff, I decided to grab a small backpack so I could have a little break from my bike whenever I wanted to go somewhere that my bike couldn't. It would be nice to have as a backup in case something were to happen to my bike, too. So, now that I have my backpack I'm ready to go climb Mt. Humphrey's Peak!

I went back out into the forest before leaving. I wanted to spend a little more time here. For a while I was following some trails but then I just wandered off into who knows where. It was really nice out there. I didn't care where I was at as long as I wasn't trespassing.

I must have wandered off ten miles from town. I had been walking my bike from noon until it was close to dark. I could no longer hear the sounds of the city. I needed to find me a good place to camp for the night. Man, that wasn't too hard. See a spot you like? There. Camp there. That's what freedom feels like!

I had my tent set up and felt very peaceful. This was a great place to relax. I didn't even feel like I needed a fire to keep me company. It was pretty cold out there but I'd be alright. I just wanted to listen to the animals of the night and let them take me away into dream land. Hopefully nothing would be waking me up out of dream land, though. It did feel pretty wild out there. Then again, that's why I always slept with my bear spray and bowie knife right next to my face.

The next day I decided to head back into town. I just wanted to grab me one last cup of coffee before heading out. I found a good trail as I was heading back towards town so it didn't take me very long to make it back.

The coffee shop had a laid-back atmosphere so I didn't mind hanging out. Most of the time I would just get my coffee and leave because people put off by anything out of the ordinary, and that means me!

Speaking of being put off, I remember sitting there enjoying my coffee when I fell into a trance of people watching. I had my sights set on this one man in particular. He was sitting on this leather couch that was in front of me and a little to the left. A perfect spot for him to be right in my peripherals. Okay. Who's starting to sound weird here now? Ha!

But, seriously, what actually caught my attention was what I overheard. He was using pick up lines to try and talk to this lady sitting beside him. She was obviously out of his league. I wanted to see how this turned out. He's talking to her for about five minutes or so and she just ups and leaves. Maybe if he had some coffee or something? It was a coffee shop after all. He had some balls, though, I'll give him that.

I'm still sitting here sipping on my coffee and I notice that he's kind of tweaking out. Like he just can't wait for another woman to sit on the couch next to him. Every time a woman would come around he would calm down and try to act cool.

Another woman takes a seat and he used the same exact approach that he used on the woman before. He used the same pick up lines and everything. Again, another woman who is obviously out of his league. She didn't stick around long either. I didn't know people watching could be so fun.

A few minutes later and a lady sits at the table just beside his arm of the couch. He immediately turns and uses the same pick up lines again! This was too funny. I felt kind of bad for the guy. Someone needs to show him how to approach women but I had other things to tend to.

I went to use the restroom before leaving and when I came back there was a $20 bill sitting next to my things with a piece of paper that read "You remind me of my son." I had no idea who left this. I looked around and didn't see anyone that was making it known to me that it was them. I felt like I owed someone a "thank you" so I just said it to whoever was listening.

I left the coffee shop and began my way up towards the mountain trail head. My bike is starting to look and feel a lot different now. I had a loaded backpack (medium sized, so it didn't look out of place) on my rear, and my new solar panel sitting on the front rack.

I forgot to mention that while I was back in town I was also picking that up. SunTactics had made me an ambassador proposal and wanted me to use their largest and latest design. I was cool with that!

My bike looked like something from the future. I literally had everything I needed and then some. This thing could take me anywhere and I wouldn't have any problems keeping my electronics charged.

Happy with my new set up, I continued on up towards Mt. Humphrey. I had a good visual of it. It did look a little intimidating. Not because of the size but because the peak still had a good amount of snow. The one thing that I didn't have was crampons. Would I need them? Only one way to find out.

As I was making my way up to the trail head I was already beginning to feel the altitude change. It was a pretty steep climb, too. Even though I was in really good shape I was still getting a bit winded. I saw a few cyclists who were coming down from the top. One of them even stopped to tell me that the ride back down is worth it, but they were shocked to see me heading up with so much gear.

I was getting pretty close to the lodge when I came around a curve and noticed a car had smashed into the safety rail. It was a Nissan Altima, just like the one I used to have before my life took a huge turn. It felt kind of like an omen. Maybe if that tree had never fallen on my car then I would have found myself in a similar situation.

At least the person driving the car was okay. He was standing back behind the car talking to a police officer. In my head I was thinking, "Maybe you would be better off on a bike, dude." I had been living off of my bike for a while and had forgotten what it was like to have to worry about things like this. It was a lot easier for sure.

I finally made my way to the ski lodge just before the trail head. I immediately asked a worker if I could lock my bike up in one of their sheds while I went to hike up the mountain. She went to ask her manager. A few minutes she returned and said that he would like to speak with me.

I followed the lady upstairs to where the manager's office was. He walked over to me and said that they couldn't keep my bike here at the lodge and that it wouldn't matter because the mountain was closed unless you had a back-country permit.

What in the world was this? I can hike a mountain any time I want! I'll go walk from somewhere else if I needed to. I didn't have time to file for some permit. Maybe I'll go talk to the forest ranger and see what he says.

I made my way over to the ranger station and asked if he would mind hanging onto my bike while I went to hike the mountain. He asked, "How long do you expect to be gone?" I replied "Maybe three tops. Tops. Just long enough to get up there and back down without any rush."

He agreed to keep my saddle bags inside of his building and that I could lock my bike up to the tree in the back.

He never asked if I had a back-country permit so I wasn't bringing it up. He then asked if I had crampons because I wouldn't be able to make it without them. I wondered if I would need them or not but there was my answer. I told him that I had a pair in my backpack. I didn't want him to tell me that I couldn't go without them. I'd know to turn around if the ice got too bad.

He shook my hand and said "Alright then. I'll see you back here in a few days. Have fun!" I proceeded to the trail head and felt like I had just cheated my way in. I knew what I was capable of, though. I made one last gear check and started my way up the trail.

Since the trail was currently closed I had the whole trail to myself. This was going to be awesome! I get to hike this mountain without having to deal with other people. Just the way I wanted it to be. Most people prefer hiking in groups, but I guess I'm just different. Of course, I am. It will be getting dark soon. Best get to moving.

I made it about a fourth of the way up the mountain before it got dark and I was already walking through snow. I didn't have my tent with me but I did have my tarp. I was trying to cut back on weight so I could make this as quick and painless as possible.

I made a quick shelter in the snow and used my tarp over the top. I dug out a large trench all around my sleeping area for the colder air to sink into. I put my sleeping pad down, got into my sleeping bag, and went right to sleep inside of my little make shift den. It was actually nice and cozy.

I heard something walking around and breaking branches while I was trying to sleep. I stayed as quiet and as still as possible. I knew that I was in black bear territory and I just had a feeling that's what it was. I wasn't too worried. I had a few snacks but they were hung up in a tree about 50 yards away.

My den was pretty much completely concealed and off away from the trail. I did worry about whatever it was walking through here and stepping on my den, though. Thankfully, that didn't happen and whatever it was continued on its way. It hung around for about thirty minutes, though.

I woke up the next morning and sure enough there were black bear tracks all around. I packed up and made my way over to my food cache. The bear had come around to check it out but everything was still there. I guess hanging my food up that night was a good decision!

I wasn't really sure where I was at this point. I accidentally wandered off of the main trail last night. I could see the trail I was supposed to be on from the map on my phone. Apparently, I had been on a game trail.

I don't guess it mattered. I knew I was heading up. I don't need a trail for that. So, I continued on just following my gut.

I was walking for about an hour when I spotted, what I assume, was the bear that had been walking around last night. He hadn't noticed me yet so I yelled at him, hoping he would bolt the other way. That worked somewhat. He ended up running in the same direction that I was heading. How wonderful.

There was a clearing between wooded sections. He ran off into those woods so I decided to follow the clearing up the rest of the way. I could see the peak from here. A straight shot up the mountain wasn't exactly the easiest idea but I'd get it done.

As I was getting closer to the top I noticed a large piece of metal. "What the heck is this and why is it up here?" Then I saw another piece. And another. And then I realized that I was looking at the wind to an airplane.

I still had service so I decided to do some research and found out that a B-24 had crashed up here back in 1944. All eight crewmen were killed during the training mission.

As it turns out a lot of people come up here looking for the site and never find it. I just so happened to stumble across it by accident. I felt privileged but at the same time I felt sadness for them and their families. Things happen, though. One way or another. I took several pictures from the wreckage, said a few words, and continued on my way to the top.

I mentioned while I was cycling up to the trail head that I felt winded. Man, I was really starting to feel it now at about 11,500 feet above sea level. I had to stop a few times to catch my breath. I was really close to the top now. The snow had turned to solid ice. The wind was blowing a good 50 mph. There were a lot of boulders to get up and around. It was getting pretty steep, too. If I fell up here I would be a goner, and falling wouldn't be too hard.

Since I had seen that bear earlier I had accidentally left the safety off of my bear spray. I had it fastened to my belt loop and when I went to step up on one of the rocks, the bear spray triggered as it smashed into my side.

The bear spray hit me directly in the face and I immediately fell to the ground. Luckily, I didn't go sliding down the mountain, but I was in so much pain. I sat there rubbing snow all over my face and trying to get my breath back. Getting my breath back was the hardest part since there wasn't very much oxygen up here to begin with.

After gathering myself from that little incident I was ready to get to the peak of this thing. As I made it to the top I realized that I had to follow these little wooden trail markers to make it to the highest point. It was super sketchy up here. It was solid ice and the wind was strong enough to slide me around. On the opposite side was a straight drop. I'd guess it was about two hundred feet down. On the side that I had just came up wasn't a straight drop but if you did start to fall then you would be in for a long ride, slamming into rocks and trees on your way.

I manage to get as close to the highest point as possible but I couldn't do it. It was just too steep and too slick. The ice was so hard that I couldn't even bust it with my machete. I was close enough to the top that I could easily throw a rock and have it land up there. This would have to do. I was satisfied.

I stood on top of the mountain, enjoying the view. I could see as far as my eyes would carry me in either direction. It was beautiful from up here. I wish I could have stayed longer but I was starting to feel the effects of altitude sickness, and decide to make my way back down. All of that hard work for thirty minutes to enjoy it. Totally worth it, though. Making it back down turned out to be a little more difficult. At least for the first 1,000 feet or so.

I had made it back down to the ski lodge in no time! I went inside to grab a slice of pizza and a beer. The lady that I spoke to the day before walked by and I said "Man, the top of Mt Humphrey was awesome!" She knew that I wasn't supposed to be up there but what was she going to do about it now? Too late now!

I went over to the ranger's station to pick up my things. He wasn't there but I left a note saying that I had made it back and thanked him for letting me take the opportunity without a back-country permit. Score one for the good guys!

I don't think they really care anyways. They just don't want to be sending people up to rescue someone who has gotten hurt. That's my point of view from it anyways. Having just been up there, I wouldn't recommend it for most people, though. I did a lot of mountain climbing while I was in the Army so I had quite a bit of experience. Only you know what you are capable of!

Riding my bike back down from the trail head was awesome. I just sat back and coasted for a good ten minutes before reaching the bottom. The cyclists that told me the ride down was worth it? They weren't kidding around. This was great!

I decided to go back into town to trade my pack in for cheaper one so I would have a little more spending money. I also, picked up some trekking poles from an outdoor store. I didn't feel like I'd need them so I returned those too.

I was able to return my backpack to the outdoor store instead of sending it back online, which saved me a lot of time. It was the same store so it didn't make any difference to them. Now that I had a little more money in my pocket and it was getting late, I decided to call around to see if I could find a really cheap motel for the night. I ended up going to The Canyon Inn where the owner offered me a free night. Wow! I got lucky!

I was walking over to my room and this lady was sitting in a chair next to hers. Looks like we're going to be neighbors for a few hours. She asked me if I wanted to come have a beer with her so I said "Sure! Just let me put my stuff up and I'll be right back out."

We talked about how I had been trekking across the United States and that I'd just come down from Mt Humphrey's Peak. She was impressed and offered me another beer. Ha! And then she started telling me how she was traveling with a band. She was a fiddler and they had just played a show here the night before. She was staying here tonight and then moving on again tomorrow.

We shared our dreams and I remember her telling me that hers was to own a yak farm. That was the first time I'd ever heard that one. She was very passionate about yaks, though. I hope that's where she is in life now.

She left to go to Walmart and asked if I needed anything. "Anything?", I asked. "Anything at all!", she replied. Jokingly, I said, "Get me something exotic."

After she leaves I walk back into my room and get myself a shower and do some laundry. Okay, I took a shower with my clothes. That's what doing laundry meant. Not that it matters but just to give you an idea. After I got cleaned up I heard a knock at the door. It was the manager of the motel and he asked me if I'd like to come have dinner with them. So, I said yes and followed him over.

We sat in the lobby and he brought us both out two large bowls of soup and some cornbread. Now, this is what I'm talking about! I got me a free room, free meal, free beer from my neighbor, and I'm just living it up. Couldn't get any better than this. But it did get better. He had a dog in the back and let me go back and there to play with him. I've always been a sucker for pups. If you're having a bad day it's like they can sense it and they'll always have your back. I'm a firm believer in calling a dog a man's best friend.

After dinner, I went back over to my hotel and the lady just got back from shopping. She said "Hey, you said you wanted something exotic, right?" I nodded and she threw a can of sour cream and onion chips at me. We both had a good laugh about that. Her sense of humor reminded me of my own.

We sat around and had a few more beers, talking the night away. I wish I would have hung caught her name and number so I could see what she's up to these days but I was just living in the moment.

The next morning, I made my way to the last gas station on the edge of town on to pick up some coffee. You've probably made the assumption by now that I really like coffee. Well, you're right. As a matter of fact, it became my motivation to get from one town to the next. It wasn't much but it gave me something short term to shoot for. If you look at just the big picture then you'll feel overwhelmed. You need to have small goals that work your way up to the main goal. That's the way I see it.

Now I'm heading towards Grand Canyon National Park. Only 75 miles to go? That should be pretty easy. I've always wanted to visit the Grand Canyon and it was a great day for riding. Clear skies, not too hot, and not too cold. Everything was perfect.

I was only maybe 30 miles or so from the Grand Canyon when I came across what looked like something straight out of The Flintstones. That's exactly what it was, actually. It was some kind of replica of the cartoon, but life size. It was pretty cool. It would cost money to enter and I wasn't that interested, but I did take a quick peek over the fence to get an idea of what I was missing out on. From the outside, though, it looked just like Fred Flintstone's house. Pretty cool! Only 19 miles from Grand Canyon now and it's starting to get dark. I went ahead and did some night riding but things got a little iffy after I spotted a mountain lion.

Coming into the Grand Canyon area there were these steep walls on either side of the road. The mountain lion had been following me for a while now. I didn't know if I should keep riding or just park it for the night. I decided to just stop and put up camp. I knew that cat was around here so I was ready for him if he decided to try and mess with me.

I made it through the night was ready to make my way into Grand Canyon. I remember this was Valentine's Day because a lot of women kept asking me to be their valentine. Ha! I don't know why but I was doing better with the ladies now than when I wasn't homeless. Maybe they just liked that wild and scruffy look. Who knows? It got me a free coffee, though!

I finally made it to the Grand Canyon and it was awesome! There were a lot of tourists here, walking around with their cameras. I was kind of in the same boat but I highly doubt we were doing it for the same reason. I was basically touring the country but there was just something different about me. I wasn't like them. I had become estranged. Even though I tried to remain presentable, something inside of me just set me apart from other people.

As I was walking around the Grand Canyon I couldn't help but want to check out the valley below. I chained my bike up to a picnic table and hiked down to the bottom. As a matter of fact, I ran down. It was a long way to go and I was ready to do some exploring

I wanted to stick around and explore the bottom of the canyon but I was worried that someone might steal my bike. I figured the chances in that were slim but it still had all of my gear on it. Even taking the time to run down was a bit risky but I had to do it!

Coming back up to the top sure was a rush. I started to feel the onset of altitude sickness. That will really give you good idea of just how massive this place really is. After I made it back to the top I noticed a sign that read something along the lines of "Do not attempt to descend and ascend the entire canyon in one day as it can cause health problems". A little late for that!

I was in really good shape so luckily, I was able to shake it off within about thirty minutes. Keep this in mind if you plan on hiking into the Grand Canyon. I probably would have done it even if I had seen the sign before hiking down, though!

I went back to the visitor center so I could fill up on water, take a little lunch break (which was just a packet of tuna and a granola bar), and then I began following the road east to get out of there.

It was starting to get pretty late. I thought about doing some night riding into Cameron but I noticed a sign that said to watch for mountain lions for the next ten miles. I decided to wait until the morning.

There was still enough daylight left for me to find a spot that I was comfortable with setting up camp. I wandered off about 100 yards from the road and began searching for my home for the night.

I found bear, elk, and mountain lion tracks. Some of the tracks were fresh and some of the poop was fresh, too. I wasn't sure that this was the best location to be in but it was too late to do anything at this point.

I put my tent up so the back was up against a large tree and then made a barrier around me using logs and sticks. I didn't make the barrier to keep anything out but at least I would hear it falling down if something got curious of my tent.

The night went on without any problems, although I did hear a lot of noises. Nothing came around my tent at least. Normally, I wouldn't have been on such high alert but after seeing all of those tracks, you can't really blame me. Morning finally came and I was on the move again.

The road brought me close to the Grand Canyon several times as I was riding along and I stopped at the pull-outs to check out all of the viewpoints. One of the stops was Duck a Rock, which basically looked like a huge duck sitting on a rock. I wonder where they came up with that name?

Another interesting site was the Desert View Watchtower. It caught my attention because I thought that it had better history to it than it actually does. From what I gathered, it was built 1932 as a rest stop. It still looks cool, though.

As I'm leaving the Desert View Watch Tower, I come around a curve and there two large bull elks. They seemed to be content with grazing but I was a little nervous seeing as how I was only 20 yards away.

I knew they could get aggressive but it became apparent that they wouldn't mind me as long as I kept at this distance. They stared at me for about a minute and then went back to eating, so I carried on around them. They must have been used to all of the people coming in and out of the park.

It was starting to get late again. I watched a beautiful sunset, spreading out orange and purple hues out over the desert. Before it got completely dark, I decided to check out some canyons. "Beware of Rattlesnakes" was the sign that I saw as I entered the trail. Sure enough, I saw a Rattlesnake. And then I saw another. Okay, I decided to just get out of there! That warning sign definitely deserved to be in its place.

I continued on through the night until I made it into Cameron, Arizona. It was pretty late when I got there and I was exhausted. I found a gas station and walked maybe a hundred feet from it. I needed some rest but didn't want to be spotted so I just threw my sleeping pad and sleeping bag on the ground.

That wasn't the best idea. Within about an hour I realized that my sleeping bag was full of spiders. I decided to go ahead and pull my tent out. Luckily, no one said anything. The next morning, I swung over to the gas station to grab me a cup of coffee. Then as I was leaving town I was about to cross a bridge when I noticed that I could get down in there and explore.

There were a lot of little caves, large crevices, and large boulders for climbing. I was out here for about two hours when I went into one of the caves and found a very defined spear head and a small piece of petrified wood. How cool! It felt like they were meant to be found but not kept so I left them there.

I was running low on water and I was completely out of food. I was burning a lot of calories but I wasn't eating much as it was. I decided it would be a good idea to make a detour into Tuba City.

On my way into Tuba City I was hit by a sand storm. It only lasted about 30 minutes but it was really intense. That was the first sand storm I had been in since I started my journey. Good thing I ha sunglasses and a bandanna with me!

I was able to fill my water up in Tuba City but I didn't have any luck with food. I knew I would be fine without food for a while but it was starting to get to me mentally. I was craving meat so bad that I began to hallucinate. I kept thinking that shrubs were deer and I would get excited. I don't guess it would have mattered if I saw a deer anyways. Not like I had a way to get one.

After I left Yuba City I rode for maybe 40 miles or so and decided that I really needed some food. I stopped to set up some snares with some steel wire that I had been hanging onto. I put my tent up and played the waiting game. I had six snares set up and I had a good feeling that I would have something pretty soon. Darkness was coming and I knew the animals would be on the move.

A couple of hours after the sun had gone down, sure enough, I heard exactly what I had been waiting for. No mistaking the sounds of a rabbit. I went and got my supper for the night and collected the rest of my snares. I only needed one and didn't want to accidentally catch another.

I started a fire and inspected my rabbit for any fleas. I was hungry but I didn't want to get sick. It appeared to be in good health so I went ahead and threw him over the fire. Not the best meal but it would last me for now.

The next day I rode into Page and got there just as the sun was setting. One of the people who was following my blog called ahead and got me a motel room. Since I ended up getting there so late they said I could stay for two nights and the owner even gave me a pizza! It felt good to be able to fill my belly, get a shower, and get some laundry done.

After I left the motel I headed over to check out the Colorado River. I noticed that Horseshoe Bend was just a few miles down the road so I had to go and check that out! I didn't even know what Horseshoe Bend was until I saw it. I've seen so many pictures of this place and I never knew where it was or what it was called. What a cool place to accidentally end up at! It's just a large bend in the Colorado River but the fact that it is somewhat of a famous location thanks to so many photographers made it really something to be there.

I went back up towards the bridge to cross over into Utah but then I noticed that I could follow a trail down and walk along the river. Nothing spectacular happened while I was walking down there but it was really beautiful and it felt so nice to be able to dip my head into the crystal-clear water.

Just on the other side of the bridge I noticed a cave up on the side of a cliff. I had to go check that out! This is right along the highway so if you were driving through you couldn't miss it. I made my way up and I immediately noticed a lot of graffiti. I'll never understand why people like to ruin these precious parts of our past with their stupid gang signs and vulgarity. Besides that, it was really cool. There was plenty of soot inside so you could tell that it was well used many years ago.

After I came back down I was making my way to claim my Utah sign. Then I ran into a man who was hitch hiking. He stopped me and asked if I knew where he could get any meth. What in the world? And he thought I was crazy for riding a bike.

It was February 20, 2015 and I just claimed my Utah sign. I was making really good time but it was about to be getting dark so I decided to look for another place to camp. It wasn't difficult to find a place to camp out here, though. All I did was walk away 50 yards from the highway and that was it. Nothing but beauty surrounded me. No lights or noises from the city, and very light traffic. It was so peaceful out here. The weather was perfect, too. I only used my tents mesh without the rain cover so I could sleep under the stars; without being attacked by a bunch of spiders again.

The next morning, I rode until about noon and I just couldn't help myself. I had to take some time off to go hiking. If you enjoy rock climbing this is the place for you! I didn't have any spotters or gear for it but I couldn't help myself. There were so many great spots to climb. I found a few tunnels in some of the formations. One of the tunnels that I made my way into had soot and carvings inside. I wished I could sit around out here all day but I needed to make it to my next water supply.

I rode until I came across a hostel that was about 50 miles from Kanab, Utah. I think the hostel was called Paria Canyon Ranch if I remember correctly. When I pulled up I didn't see anyone anywhere. I sat at one of the picnic tables for about an hour and still no sign of anyone. I decided to go ahead and put my tent up because it was starting to get dark.

As soon as I had my tent put up I heard what sounded

like a small engine. I stood up and saw a guy coming over on a four-wheeler. "What are you doing?", he asked. He sounded angry that I had set my tent up. I replied, "I didn't feel like night riding into Kanab and this seemed like a pretty good place to camp. I've been sitting out here for almost two hours and I didn't see anyone."

He said he didn't mind if I camped out here in my tent but said it would be five dollars. I had been collecting change that I saw while I was riding so I counted out $5. I guess he noticed that I was pretty bad off on cash and asked if I'd like to help him load some old junk up for $50. So, I did. He said I could go into the hostel if I wanted to look around. I could use the restroom and shower if I wanted, or the kitchen if I had any food that I would like to heat up.

The inside of the hostel looked like something straight out of a western movie. It had an eerie vibe to it, also. Maybe it was because I was in there by myself, lights off, and walking around like a weirdo with my headlamp. I walked back outside and saw two people standing on the porch. They had been in the cheaper part of the hostel that was next to the building I just came out of. They invited into their room and then we talked for a few hours while sharing some beers.

I went back out to my tent after hanging out with this couple fell asleep pretty quick. When I woke up I peeked my head out like I always do but his time I saw that it had snowed. I love riding in the snow so this was going to be a good day! Not too many people can say that.

I went back into the hostel and took that offer up on the shower. Then I packed up and made my way for Kanab. I had a care package on the way but it wouldn't be there until tomorrow so I wasn't in a rush, but I did get there earlier than I intended.

I looked for a cheap motel and decided to swing by the Aikens Lodge. I got the room for $20 so I was pretty happy with that. Nothing fancy but I just wanted a place to wait out this package that was on the way.

It was still pretty early so I decided to head over to McDonald's to grab something off of the dollar menu. When I got there, the couple that I had ran into back at the hostel was there too. They were driving across the country but it still felt good to talk with travelers however they had chosen to do so.

After we parted ways I went back to my motel and took a nice hot bath. Actually, it wasn't that nice of a bath. It turned out that my room was for people with a handicap, so the bath tub was really small. As a matter of fact, I don't think you were supposed to even take a bath in it. Ha! Whatever works?

The next morning, I head over to the post office to pick up my care package from Jody. The post office refused to give me my packages because I had it sent there as general delivery. This is the first time that I've ever had that happen. I'm pretty sure it was illegal for them to charge me shipping on a package that already had the shipping paid for.

Either way, I went ahead and gave them $30 for my packages. There was well more than $30 worth of stuff in there and I wasn't going to have the package turned back around. I tried explaining the whole situation to the lady at the post office but she was hard headed and irritable. Luckily, Jody sent about ten pounds of food along with $40 so I was good to go for a while.

I went back to the motel and talked to the owner about what had happened. I'm not sure why but he offered me a free night if I wanted it. I took him up on that offer! I spent the rest of the day lying in bed, watching the news to try and catch up on what's been going on in the world.

The next morning, I was all charged up and ready to go. Then I passed by a music store. I couldn't help but stop in and play on a guitar for a few minutes. It had been a while since I was able to play. A little bit of nostalgia was a great boost but it also made me miss the old days.

Making my way up towards Mt Carmel Junction was a short but serene ride. I finally made it and was hoping to go into Zion National Park but they had a fee so I turned it down. I regret not going in so I'll just have to add that to my bucket list.

Although, I didn't go into the National Park I did go back as far as I could. I wandered off into the woods and found a place to camp. After I had everything set up I went for a hike and it turned out to be pretty nice, so I couldn't complain.

The next morning, I went down to this restaurant that had a sign with a woman holding a pie. The sign read "Home of the Ho-Made Pies". I thought that was pretty funny. I went inside to grab a cup of coffee because it had gotten really cold that night.

I wanted to warm up so I sat inside to drink my coffee when someone asked, "Did you camp out there last night?" I said that I did and he said, "Wow, man. You must have some really good gear. It got down to 10 degrees last night." I laughed and said, "Yeah, it did feel a little cold now that you mention it." That was good news to me, though. I knew if I had no problems at zero degrees then I was doing pretty good!

I went outside and realized that I had a flat. It had been a while since I'd had a flat. These Schwalbe Marathon Plus tires were really worth the money! As I was fixing my flat a van pulls up and a bunch of people jumped out.

They asked if I'd like to come traveling with them but I explained how I was heading up to Alaska. Then they noticed my solar panels and showed me the solar panels they had on top of their van. I can't remember exactly what the solar panels did but I noticed they had a bunch of vegetables growing inside so I'm guessing they were powering UV lights. They also said they used vegetable oil to power their vehicle. Interesting group of people that I could see myself hanging with but I had other plans.

I finally made my way into Panguitch and stopped by a

motel to see if they had any work I could do in exchange for a room. Surprisingly, the manager said yes! She said they were getting new furniture in and there were a few rooms that still had old furniture that needed to be moved out.

I moved all of the furniture out of three rooms into a storage area and then she gave me the keys to a room. That was a pretty sweet deal! About an hour later she came to the room that I was in and gave me a pizza and some cheese sticks. Total score! I was set for the night!

The next morning, I was on my way again. As I was getting close to Junction I decided to take a dirt road that went back to a mountain. As I got closer to the mountain I noticed the weather was starting to pick up. The sky darkened, the wind picked up, and then all of a sudden, I found myself in the middle of a blizzard.

I turned to make my way back to the main road but it was a slow process. I ended up having to get off of my bike and walk it because I couldn't see anything. I began to wonder what I had gotten myself into. If this storm doesn't blow over quick then I'm going to find myself in a mess. I'm probably 15 miles from the highway. The snow was coming from every direction. There was no way to turn your back to it.

I kept my head down and kept walking until I made it back to the road. Nearly a foot of snow had fallen during the time it took me to make it back. Luckily, the worst of the storm was fairly localized. It was probably 18 more miles of fighting my way through the snow before I made it into Circleville.

The snow was still heavy but at least the wind had calmed down significantly. I decided to push on through it into Junction. There wasn't much in Junction but I found an awning to stand under for a few minutes to get out of the snow. I didn't feel like just sitting there, though. I was actually enjoying the snow for some crazy reason. I threw some zip ties on my tires for traction and rode up until the snow backed off (which was another 30 miles).

After all of the snow had backed off I was riding through a mountainous area. There were steep inclines on either side of the highway so I was basically riding through a canyon for quite a while.

This car passes me from behind and then about a mile up ahead I see the same car facing my direction. I noticed the driver is pointing a camera at me so I stop and point my phone at him like I'm taking his picture and then he speeds off. No idea what that was about but it kind of freaked me out being out there so far between towns and basically trapped within these mountains. Creeper.

Anyways, the snow picks up again but I finally made it to this restaurant called Hoover's Restaurant and got me a nice lunch. The waitress told me the meal was on the house so that was a plus! I had plenty of food from the package Jody sent but I just wanted something hot a filling so this was a really nice gift.

I then made my way as far as I could before it got dark. I didn't want to be anywhere near the road in case that weird guy came back looking for me, so I walked my bike up over a few hills and found a great spot to camp. I could oversee everything. Mountains in everything direction and a beautiful sunset to end it all off with it.

The next morning, I pack up and ride about 30 miles into Joseph. When I got there, I found a little store to get me some coffee. They asked me if I was cold. I kind of laughed and said, "I'm not but my feet are!" So, this lady goes to the back and brings me a chair. She tells me to sit in front of the fire place and warm my feet up.

I stayed in the store longer than I intended. I guess I got a little too comfortable with that furnace. We ended up talking about all kinds of things too. It was nice to be able to just sit and have some good conversation, but it was starting to get late and I needed to go find me a place to camp.

I didn't have to go too far. There was an old truck stop

so I just sat my tent up in the back. I was close to the highway so getting started in the morning should be easy enough. I am starting to get kind of bored of this bike, though.

The next morning was March 1, 2015 and I decided to go ahead and put my bike up for sale on my blog. I knew it wouldn't sell automatically but this should give me plenty of time. I would be making it to the loneliest highway soon and I had some different plans for that!

I was stoked to finally make it up to highway 50. This was the day that I had been waiting for. Someone bought my bike. I used that money to order a backpack. I was going to be walking the rest of the way and I was super excited! I just had to make it to Delta, which was about three days away. Everything was working out perfectly.

Those next three days were spent taking it pretty slow. I didn't need to be in Delta too soon or my backpack wouldn't be there. I did maybe 20 miles and wandered off to find a nice place to camp. That night when I was camping I decided to make a fire. Not only was it cold but it also felt like it gave me some company. For supper, I ended up mixing a couple packs of tuna with some beef jerky. I heated them up in a collapsible pan that Skip gave me back in Flagstaff. It had served me well on a few occasions.

I went ahead and used one of my canteens to heat up some coffee, too. When you're on the move you don't really need to try to stay warm. Your body will do most of the work for you. When you're stationary, however, a hot meal can do wonders. Nothing like going to bed with a warm belly on a cold night.

I finally reached a sign that read, "28 Miles to Delta". I figured I would go ahead and get into town and be there to grab my new backpack the next day. On my way into Delta I noticed a large black horse off in the distance. She was running for me at full speed so I stopped and walked up to the fence line. Once she made her way over, she began reaching out at me; as if she wanted to eat my hat. I leaned in a little closer to see what she wanted. It felt like she was giving me kisses so I asked, "What? You want a kiss?" and she tilted her head down. I kissed her on the end of her nose and then backed away. She started running around in circles and then followed me as far as she could.

As I was coming into Delta a lady in a van pulls over and asks if I need a ride. I said that I was just heading into Delta so it wasn't a problem. I was only maybe 5 miles away and it wasn't a big deal for me, but she insisted. She felt bad because I was out in the rain, so we put my bike in the back and I let her drive me into town. After I told her what I was doing she offered to get me a motel room. She said she would let me stay at her house but I couldn't because I wasn't Mormon. I was totally down for a motel, though!

After she dropped me off she asked if it would be okay for her and her family to come by in the morning to talk to me about Mormonism. I figured that would be a fair trade but I never saw her again. I always got up really early so I may have already been gone when they got there; if they even did.

I went straight down to the post office and got the backpack that I had been dreaming of since day one. I don't know why it took me so long to make the switch but here it was! It was an Osprey Aether 70 and I immediately fell in love with it. I named her "Bessy the Back Breaker". It was a fitting name, I thought. The guy who bought my bike was all the way back in Pennsylvania. Thank goodness, he also paid for the shipping or I would have had to stick around in Delta looking for some odd jobs.

Going from a twenty mile per hour pace down to a three mile per hour pace felt really great. People thought that I was crazy before but now they're really starting to wonder. Why would I decide to switch to a backpack just as I'm getting ready to go through the loneliest highway in Nevada?

Well, besides the fact that walking was my initial plan, I wanted the challenge. I felt like I was physically capable of it. Mentally, though? This is exactly what I needed. When you have fifty to eighty pounds of weight on your back and 100 miles between water sources, you will suck it up or you will die. If that doesn't motivate you then maybe you better get motivated.

Besides all of that, I planned on backpacking into Alaska and I needed to take some time to get used to it. This was exactly what I felt that I needed to make the change. There's no giving up when you're in the middle of the desert. You can't just call it quits. You have to fight for it. I needed that.

From Delta to Hinckley was only about 8 miles. That was easy. Then I had 153 miles to Ely, Nevada. Things were about to get real serious really quick. I made sure to hydrate as much as I could before I left Delta and had about 3 gallons worth of water. It added a lot of weight but I wouldn't let it slow me down. Keep in mind that this around the beginning of March, so heat wasn't an issue yet. At least I had that going in my favor.

It wasn't too far outside of Hinckley when I came across a tree that was covered in shoes. I'm not sure what that was about but I figured it was something that travelers had done. I wished that I had an extra shoe to throw up into it but I kind of needed mine right now.

5

I noticed every now and then that a beer bottle would be sticking out of the ground, as if it had been planted. The top would be pushed down and the bottom sticking up. I saw quite a few so this was obviously no accident. I found me a beer bottle and carried it for a few miles and then I planted one of my own. If you're ever traveling through here be prepared to carry on at least one of these legacies because there isn't much else going on out here and people like me will appreciate the little things.

It was starting to get dark so I decided to go ahead and put up camp for the night. I didn't exactly get an early start anyways. Hopefully tomorrow I will be crossing into Nevada. It sure was peaceful camping out here. I'm not sure when exactly they consider this to turn into the loneliest highway but it sure was lonely, and I loved it.

I thought there was supposed to be a lake out here? Sevier Lake? I never saw a lake, though. It was probably dried up like everything else out here. I might have gotten some mud out of it if I walked out far enough but I figured I would pass that up and keep on walking. It was getting dark again but I decided I had better just keep walking. I still had a long way to go before my next water supply.

It was really peaceful walking out here during the night. The moon was so bright that I didn't even use my headlamp, unless I heard something creeping around. I never saw too many animals out here, though. I had a fox following me for a while but he wasn't bothering anything. Just curious I suppose.

I finally crossed into Nevada that morning and turned to see a sign that said 96 miles to Delta. I had been making some really good time! By late that afternoon I reached another sign that said 56 miles to Ely. I figured I would go ahead and walk another night. I was starting to get kind of low on water anyways. You don't need to drink as much water when the sun isn't beaming down on you.

I finally made it into Ely the next day around noon. Man, I was starting to feel tired but at least I made it here and I could hydrate all day long, and that's exactly what I did. Then the next morning I drank more water and made sure that my urine was clear. I emptied myself, drank another gallon, filled up my hydration pack and canteens, and I was off to Eureka. It was 80 miles to Eureka and I got an early start. I should be able to make it there by tomorrow afternoon if I don't take too many breaks. Not that I was in a hurry. Not exactly.

I know that you can sit and make it a few days without water but not while you're exerting yourself the way that I was. It was day three between Eureka and Fallon and I was only able to make 20 miles. I thought I was making better mileage but out here it's really hard to tell.

The next day I saw a sign that said 79 miles to Fallon. My timing got all out of whack. I should have done more night walking but my feet just weren't up to it. I should have pushed myself harder. I guess I'll have to!

Thankfully, a truck passes by. It was pretty rare to see any vehicles out here. I saw them stop and start to back up. It was an older man and woman and asked if I needed a ride. I told them that I was trying to walk the rest of it but would asked if they had any water on them.

They didn't have any water and insisted that I let them take me into Fallon, so I agreed. I might not have another chance if things got any worse. I was thankful that they stopped, as hard headed as I was about getting in. It actually turned out to be a really nice ride, anyways. The conversation was nice and I felt like I had made some friends. They admired what I was doing but we agreed that there's nothing wrong with accepting some help when you know you've done all you can do.

We saw some wild horses fighting while we were driving and stopped to watch them for about thirty minutes or so. Then we made our way on into Fallon. It sure seemed like a short drive. After we made it into Fallon the couple gave me $40 and dropped me off at Walmart.

I decided to go on in and pick me up a new tripod. I grabbed the cheapest one that I could find. I had an okay camera but I hated just taking pictures right up in front of my face, or not being in the pictures at all. I was running a blog, after all, and I wanted to be able to document everything as best I could.

I decided to get a motel room while I was in Fallon, too. I ended up getting the room for $20 after talking to the manager. I really needed a shower and to get some laundry done. I needed to hydrate, too.

I sat outside of my room for the rest of the day and brought my clothes out to dry. I made a little clothes line with two chairs and some paracord. There was a lady about my age at the room next to me. She seemed really upset so I tried to talk to her but she just started screaming at me. Calm down, now. Just trying to be nice!

The next morning, I knew that I would be heading off into the desert so I made sure to be a little more prepared with my water situation. I picked up an extra gallon of water and tied it down to the back of my pack. I was ready now! I looked at my map before I left and noticed that if I walked through the desert, instead of taking the road, that

I would be able to shave off a few miles. So, that's what I would do.

I followed some back roads out of Fallon until it turned into an old service road. That eventually turned into a small dirt trail and before I knew it I was making my own trail off into the desert. It felt kind of like a bad idea but I had gained my energy back, my feet weren't sore anymore, and I had an extra gallon of water.

I just kept heading west. I knew that I would come back out to the highway eventually. While I was walking I came across an old grave site. It was just four large logs in the shape of a square. No telling how long it had been there.

After about 20 more miles or so I noticed this large circle in the ground. It was probably thirty feet across or so. There were a few rocks near the center that didn't look like any of the other rocks in the area. That immediately got my attention.

I walked around and found a few more rocks like I had seen inside of the circle. I wondered if they were meteorites. The hose on my hydration bladder had a magnet on it so you could hook it to your chest strap. The magnet stuck right to them. Now I'm really wondering if these are meteorites! I decided to go ahead and put up camp here so I could continue to investigate the area.

I ended up finding about fifty of these odd rocks, or meteorites, or whatever they were and hid them all in a pile. I knew if they were meteorites then they would be worth something so I made a note of where I put them. I've yet to go back to that location but I'm sure they're still there.

I accidentally came out on some government property. I'm not really sure how that happened. I guess they didn't expect people to be walking through the desert but I needed to find a way out of there. There was a fence blocking me from getting back onto the road.

I backtracked through the Lahontan State Recreation

Area and found a small community. There may have been ten small houses out here and the people outside were looking at me kind of funny. Not every day you see someone pop out from the desert I guess.

Anyways, I finally made it back to the highway just as the sun was going down and started making my way for Dayton. I didn't want to get into town after dark, though, so I walked until I had about 10 miles left. Then I wandered off about fifty yards from the highway and found a place to put up camp.

It was probably 2:00 am when I woke to the sound of four wheelers. What in the world were these people doing out here and at this time of night? I could see three of them all with their headlights on. I was hoping they wouldn't see my tent and come over. They got pretty close but I don't think they ever noticed me. They finally left out of there after about an hour.

At least now I should be able to get a couple of hours of sleep before the sun came up. The sun was my alarm clock. When it came up so did I. Hopefully, I would be able to find some coffee once I made it into Dayton.

I was packed up and ready to move at the crack of dawn. I made my way back over to the road and started walking. After I walked about 5 miles or so I notice this old man walking towards me on the opposite side of the street.

He had a long beard and was wearing all camouflage. As he got closer I realized that he was playing a flute. Well, that was a new one for me.

I kind of wanted to go talk to him but he was probably in his own little world like I was.

As I was coming into Dayton I noticed what appeared to be a small cave. I had to go check it out! It had a small entrance but the inside was probably large enough for ten people to gather. There was also a lot of soot in this cave as well. I always liked finding stuff like this.

Once into town I was able to find a coffee shop. As

soon as I put my bag down someone asked where I was heading and when I told them "Alaska" they offered to buy me my coffee and even gave me $10. After I had my coffee I filled up on water again and made my way for Carson City.

I had a new pack from Osprey waiting for me in Carson City but I also had a letter that wouldn't be there for a few days. This was going to be great. Maybe taking a few days to hang around would be fun. One of the people following my blog was living in Carson City and said that I could hang out with them.

Just outside of the city limits a large, black SUV pulls up beside me. There's a man about my age inside. He asked where I was going and I told him the post office. He told me to get in and he'd give me a ride.

We started talking and it got brought up that I was an Army veteran and he told me that he was in the Air Force. He didn't come off as the Air Force type, though. He seemed really uptight. He was dressed in all black and never removed his sunglasses. I was beginning to wonder if I was in the car with some kind of Secret Service agent.

After he dropped me off at the post office I looked back to check out his license plate and it was blacked out. He noticed me looking at his license plate and then he drove off.

Well, that was pretty weird but at least he's gone and I get to go try on my new pack. I needed to swap the one that I had out with a small. The medium was just too long for my torso, so I had been carrying most of the weight on my shoulders and my butt. The small fit much better!

Now I needed to go find that guy that said I could hang out with him at his bar. I can't remember his name but when I got there he let me get a shower so we could get ready to go to this bar. Man, that shower felt great! Then we went out to the bar and they said all of my drinks were on the house.

He was still working but I was ready to turn in. He said

I was welcome to go back to his apartment to crash for the night. Sounded good to me. I made my way back and as soon as I got there I crashed on the couch.

The next morning, I decided to go check out the town. I walked around until it was time for lunch. I needed to find a place to grab a bite. I came across this restaurant called "Reds Old 395". As I was sitting down waiting to order, I noticed several waitresses kept peeking around the corner at me.

Eventually, one of them walks over and asks, "Are you Jake?". When I told her that I was, she said she thought so but wanted to be sure before offering me a free lunch. I got lucky again! I'm not sure how I always ended up at just the right place at the right time.

After I left there I ran into a lady name Melissa, who had also been following my blog. She invited me over to her place and we had a couple of beers. We talked for about two hours before she said she needed to go do something, but before she left she offered to get me a motel for the night!

This was great because the day was still pretty early. That meant that I would get to walk around without my pack on. That's when I saw one of the strangest cloud formations that I had ever seen. There were four, large, dark circles; sitting and spinning right over Carson City. I decided to go back to my motel.

The next morning, I begin walking around, trying to decide on where I want to eat breakfast. I sat down in a parking lot so I could look the GPS on my phone to see what kind of restaurants I could pull up.

I noticed someone was walking over towards me but I didn't pay too much attention until she had gotten pretty close. When I looked up she said "Hey! I thought you might like some breakfast." I replied "Oh, wow! Yeah! That's actually what I was just looking for! Thank you!"

If it was up to me I would have chosen something different but you can't complain about a free meal unless it's spoiled. After I ate I went over the restaurant and paid for it anyways. I had the money to cover it and even give her a tip. She tried to give me my money back but I wouldn't take it.

After that, I decided to make my way into the mountains just on the west side of town. I walked around back there until it got dark and then I found a nice place to sit, so I could just look down at the city.

Then I noticed a ball of light coming out of the mountains on the north side of town. At first, I thought it was a plane but then I realized that it was just sitting there. What was I looking at? Maybe it was a drone? That made sense until what I saw next.

The light sits over the hills on the northwest side of town for about 10 minutes or so and then it slowly begins to move over Carson City. It sits directly over the town for about 5 minutes and then it disappears.

Then another light comes up from about the same location and does pretty much the same thing. It hovered just over the hills, went over the town, and disappeared in the same spot. And then another one!

About 5 minutes later the three lights all reappear in the spot that they disappeared in. They separate and begin slowly circling the town. They eventually stopped and met back up where they had started and formed one solid ball of light, but it never got any larger in size.

It sat there for about a minute and then it kind of did a crisscross motion and then went back down on the opposite side of town. I was pretty convinced that I had just witnessed a UFO. I was recording it on my camera and immediately transferred the video over to my phone so I could upload it to my blog.

A lot of people saw it and they were just as stumped as I was. I was going to camp up here that night but I didn't know if it was such a good idea, so I made my way back down into town and ended up sleeping in parking lot. I threw my sleeping bag down between two highway maintenance vehicles. I was too tired to put in any more effort in finding a better location. No one would see me here at least.

I was hoping that my letter would be here today but it wasn't. I didn't feel like being in the city anymore so I grabbed a cup of coffee from a gas station and then made my way back up into the mountains.

I hiked around all day and found a nice spot to camp. I hadn't put my tent up yet or anything. I just wanted to sit there and relax for a while. As I was sitting there I heard something coming up over the hill from behind where I was sitting.

It was a man. He walked over to me and we talked for a minute. I can't remember exactly what we talked about but I thought that it was strange to see this man out here. I hadn't seen anyone else all day and he didn't dress the part for someone to be out hiking. He had that same eerie presence about him as the guy I had first met when I was coming into town a few days ago.

He walked around the hill to where I couldn't see him anymore. I got suspicious and decided to walk around to see if he was heading down into the city. I didn't see him anywhere. That was odd.

I went back to sit in my spot and pulled out some beef jerky to snack on as I waited for the sun to set, then I would put my tent up. While I was sitting there eating I noticed four kids walking on the hill across from me. They stopped walking and then I blacked out.

When I came to I felt really confused. All I could see was black so I started to panic. I moved around, trying to figure out where I was and what was going on. When I got turned around I noticed a bright red light shooting up into the night sky.

I soon realized that I was lying in a ditch on the side of a dirt road. I began checking to make sure that I hadn't been hurt or mugged. Everything seemed to be there and I didn't notice any pain. I did notice that one of my trekking poles was bent, though.

I pulled my phone out and noticed that it was 3:00 in the morning. I didn't know where I was so I looked up my location on my GPS. Somehow, I had ended up several miles on the other side of Carson City, just beyond the river.

I began walking back into town so I could get my mail and get out of there. I took me all day to get back into town because I kept feeling sick and had to take a lot of breaks. I made it to the post office just before they closed, got my letter, filled up on water, and started making my way out of there.

It was starting to get late and I wondered if I wanted to stick around for another night. I just wanted to get away from Carson City, though, so I got back onto the road and continued walking.

I thought that I was in the clear from everything that had gone bizarre but it wasn't over yet. The sun had gone down but it wasn't completely dark yet. It was in that twilight phase where everything just has a subtle glow to it.

Well, I check out the time on my phone and it says that it's about 7:00 pm. I put my phone back into my pocket and walk a couple of miles. Something just didn't feel right. It should be dark by now.

I felt my phone vibrate so I pulled my phone out to check and see what it was. It was Jody, and he had sent me a picture message of the sunrise back in Arizona and said "Good morning!".

I thought he was trying to be funny but then a lot of other people began commenting on my blog, saying the same thing. I was starting to feel disoriented at this point.

I turned my phone off and turned it back on because I was wondering if something had messed up with it. When my phone came back on it said that it was 7:00 am. What in the world? It never even got dark. How is this possible? The sun should be going down but it starts coming up.

I never even missed a step. I never laid down to take a

nap or anything. I just left the post office a couple of hours ago. This just doesn't make any sense.

I began to feel really hot and then I got dizzy. I was so dizzy that I had to sit down because I felt like I was going to fall over. I made my way over to some bushes so I could lay down without anyone stopping to talk to me. That's when I vomited and passed out.

I woke up a few hours later and felt fine again. Man, I was getting out of here! Only 25 miles to Lake Tahoe. I'll be making that in no time as long as nothing like this happens again.

As I was walking along the highway this man stops and asks if I wanted a ride. At first, I said, "No. Thanks, though. I'm walking across America and I don't take rides unless I really have to." He told me to at least let him drive me to the top of the mountain and I agreed to it. I just wanted to get away from Carson City and he seemed like a cool guy. I still talk to him to this day, actually.

When he let me out I noticed a bear crossing sign. Oh, what joy! I wasn't really too worried about bears but it was the first time I had ever seen a crossing sign for them. I noticed the land had really taken a change from Carson City to Lake Tahoe. Just one mountain separated the forest from the desert. It felt great to be back with the trees again. I could see the lake up ahead and the water brought a sense of peace that I hadn't felt in a while. I was back in my safe zone.

As I was making my way down towards the lake I noticed the pine cones were super huge! I picked one up to get a picture with it and it was the size of my head! Not that I have a big head or anything. Ha! I've never seen pine cones so big, though. I thought it was pretty awesome.

When I got down to the lake I reached for my camera when I realized it was missing. The last time I remembered seeing it was when I recorded that video back in Carson City, and I wasn't going back for that; or anything else for that matter. My phone would just have to do for now.

I walked along a trail that followed along the lake for several miles. It was getting late again and the sunset was spectacular. I put my tent up just off of the trail as fast as I could so I wouldn't have to worry about it later. Then I sat and watched the sun go down.

I got up pretty early and watched the sunrise, too. It was a nice and cool start to my day. Now, I just had my sights set on crossing over in California. I wasn't in any rush, though. It was a beautiful day and I loved walking along the lake.

I made it up to Incline Village when I noticed a wallet and cell phone sitting on the side of the road. I opened up the wallet to see if there was an ID inside. It belonged to a lady who lived Vermont. That's a long way from home so I immediately called the police.

I sat around and waited for an officer to arrive. When she got there, I gave her the items, my name, and my phone number. She said she would call me as soon as she found out who the items belonged to. It was definitely out of the ordinary to find something like this, especially when the person was from the other side of the country.

About an hour later I received a phone call from the police station. They found the owner. She had recently moved to California and said her phone and wallet had been missing for several days. It was a good thing the wrong person didn't come along and swipe these things up. I was glad to have helped!

I continued walking for about an hour and finally claimed my California sign. This was awesome! I had unofficially made it across the United States. Now I just needed to make it to the coast to make it official. I still had a good way to go.

I ended my first day in California between Kings Beach and Truckee. I probably could have made it into Truckee before nightfall but I wandered off into the woods and stayed out there for quite a while.

I saw a cinnamon colored black bear while I was hiking

out in the woods here. It saw me but it didn't run towards me or away. It wasn't interested but it wasn't scared either. I kind of wished that it was. I wouldn't be sleeping lightly tonight.

I always had my bear spray ready but I felt a little intimidated, even though I hadn't seen the bear since about an hour ago. I made my way back closer to road, since I had wandered pretty far back, and set up my tent. Just for peace of mind, if nothing else, I took out my knife and taped it onto the end of my trekking pole.

I gave it a few stabs into a tree to make sure it was secure. I felt confident enough that it would help just a little bit if the situation called for it. Luckily, I never saw the bear again but I did hear branches snapping during the night. It could have been anything but when you know there's a bear around, everything sounds like a bear.

I made my way into Truckee the next morning and continued on until I reached Donner Memorial State Park. I saw a ski resort and decided to stop by for lunch and a couple of beers. The people here said they had been following my blog and offered to pay for my meal. Another great score!

I almost made it to Donner Lake before dark but I'd have to camp and get there in the morning. I'm not sure how many miles I had covered but I was making really good time now. Fifty miles a day was no longer an issue. Later on, I even got accused of taking rides because I was making such good time. Fifty miles from sunrise to sunset and then night walking, too. You can really rack up some miles.

Once I made it down to Donner Lake I headed straight over to the monument, which was a large statue made of stones with a man, woman, and child standing on top. It read,

"NEAR THIS SPOT STOOD THE BREEN CABIN OF THE PARTY OF EMIGRANTS WHO STARTED FOR CALIFORNIA FROM SPRINGFIELD,

ILLINOIS, IN APRIL, 1846, UNDER THE LEADERSHIP OF CAPTAIN GEORGE DONNER. DELAYS OCCURRED AND WHEN THE PARTY REACHED THIS LOCALITY, ON OCTOBER 29, THE TRUCKEE PASS EMIGRANT ROAD WAS CONCEALED BY SNOW. THE HEIGHT OF THE SHAFT OF THE MONUMENT INDICATES THE DEPTH OF THE SNOW, WHICH WAS TWENTY-TWO FEET. AFTER FUTILE EFFORTS TO CROSS THE SUMMIT, THE PARTY WAS COMPELLED TO ENCAMP FOR THE WINTER. THE GRAVES CABIN WAS SITUATED ABOUT THREE-QUARTERS OF A MILE TO THE EASTWARD, THE MURPHY CABIN ABOUT TWO HUNDRED YARDS SOUTHWEST OF THE MONUMENT, AND THE DONNER TENTS WERE AT THE HEAD OF ALDER CREEK. NINETY PEOPLE WERE IN THE PARTY AND FORTY-TWO PERISHED, MOST OF THEM FROM STARVATION AND EXPOSURE."

Luckily for me, the snow had come light this year. I was actually worried about making my way through here when I first started. I never really knew if I was going to be coming through here or not but it was definitely a point of interest, and since it had become in line with my route I was able to knock this one off of my bucket list. A beautiful lake, but a very harsh bit of history.

I camped off in the woods behind the lake and then the next morning I was back to walking again. From there all the way up until Grass Valley there wasn't really much going on. Just a whole lot of nature walking since the highway turned into an interstate.

I really enjoyed making my own trail through the forest, though. I found a lot of amazing camping spots and the weather was perfect. It was snowing a little bit but it wasn't enough to be bothersome. Just the right amount.

I was walking through the woods for a while and I eventually found my way back to a road. I'm not sure what road it was but I found a memorial while I was walking down it.

It was about a lady named Susan Cooley Gilliom. She was an artist that lived next to the river. She was a painter, photographer, and activist to help preserve this land.

I wasn't surprised that she would have chosen this location to focus all of her work. It was really beautiful. The river, the rocks, the trees. It all fell together in a very artistic way.

The spot is known as Susan's Spot. I don't remember it's exact location, as I was making my way through the woods when I found it; but if you wanted to look into it I'm sure you could find it. I think it was about 40 miles or so from Grass Valley, because I did come across a distance sign at one point and I remember it saying 30 miles to Grass Valley.

Those 30 miles into Grass Valley were pretty intense. A lot of hills and very dense forest. I had a lot of energy come over me and I force hiked most of it. I actually put an app on my phone to check my speed and it said I was averaging 6 miles per hour. I had camped back near Susan's Spot so I had an early start to the day and I made it into Grass Valley in time for lunch.

Just a few miles before Grass Valley a man stopped and asked if I wanted a ride into town but I told him I was fine. He said, "Well, here's $20. When you get up here a little way you'll come into Nevada City. There's a pizza place. It's one of my favorites. Swing by there and get you something." I took the man's word and found the pizza place. As I was looking at the menu I became confused because I'd never heard of any of this stuff. It turned out to be a vegan restaurant and this was new to me.

I asked the lady at the register if they had something, maybe like a pepperoni pizza? Man, don't ever walk into a vegan place and ask for something like that. The lady gave me a cheese-like pizza. I'm not sure what it was but it wasn't bad. When I got finished eating, my friend back from Texas gave me a call. While I was on the phone someone had the nerve to ask me to leave because I was taking up space since I was no longer eating. I told my friend on the phone, "Hold on. I have to go outside. These vegans are making me leave."

Okay, maybe I should have chosen my words a bit more carefully. Everyone in the restaurant started shouting, "VEGAN PEOPLE, BRO? REALLY? VEGAN PEOPLE? BRO? VEGAN? DUDE?" I swear I was about ready to punch this one guy. He was barking up the wrong tree. I didn't mean to offend them. I thought they were supposed to be proud of being vegan? Maybe he had forgotten about how he had just told me I was taking up space?

I took my things and my conversation outside. My friend, Rob, was laughing because he had heard the whole thing. It was a bit ridiculous.

He said that he'd like to join me once I made it into Sacramento and walk up the rest of the coast. I was pretty excited about having some company. He said to let him know when I was getting closer and he would get a bus ticket. I told him that I'd let him know a few days ahead so he could get everything in advance, so the ticket would be cheaper for him.

I took my time getting into Grass Valley and ended up getting there as it was getting dark. I hated coming into new towns when I couldn't really examine the area first. I ended up finding an alley between two fences. There was just enough space for me to lay my sleeping pad and sleeping bag. I hunkered down here for the night. No idea what tomorrow would have in store. I didn't really care too much at this point, though. I had become wild and now I was in the city.

If you remember, I said earlier that I had this dating site set up. I hadn't used it since that day back in Flagstaff, Arizona. I decided to change my zip code on there to see if I could find any females that would want to hang out since

I knew my chances of finding a lady who was into hiking was pretty good around these parts.

I ended up getting a message from a girl, Megan, and we started talking. She said that she would be interested in hiking with me. We planned on meeting in Auburn, California in a couple of days, so that gave me something to look forward to. I knew that I could get there by the next day if I wanted so I figured I would hang around Grass Valley and see what I could get into.

I found a hiking trail that went up over the town and decided to hide all of my gear here so I wouldn't have to lug it around everywhere. I just wanted to take a day off and relax.

I put my tent up and put all my gear inside of it. Then I completely covered my tent in brown pine needles. It sounds ridiculous but if you saw it you would be impressed. Hell, even I was impressed. It just looked like part of hill I had set it up against. Unless someone ran off the trail and smacked into it they would never even know it was there.

After I had my things put away I made my way down into Grass Valley. I ran into a guy who was pan handling with a guitar so I asked if I could join him. I played guitar and he sang. We made a pretty good team.

We played for about two hours and made $80. I took $40 from that and then I left him to his thing. Then I decided to walk over to this bar that I had seen down the street. I felt like having a few beers and just taking it easy today.

I ended up meeting this couple there who had heard about me and offered to buy me a round of drinks. So, that was a plus. I just made forty bucks and it was nice to be able to hang onto it. I told them I didn't mind paying for it but they insisted.

They ended up getting me quite a few beers. Apparently, this was a bar where you're supposed to have maybe one or two beers because they cut me off after like five. That was fine but I thought it was kind of strange. I can handle way more than five beers and I wasn't bothering anyone. I decided to go back up to my spot and just hang out by myself.

The next morning, I was packed up and ready to leave. Before I left I decided to swing by that bar for one more beer. I took my beer to the outside patio and overheard a worker say, "only allow that guy with a green bandanna one beer". I thought it was funny but, hey, that's all I wanted anyways!

I made my way into Auburn to meet up with Megan. I made it a couple of hours before she did. When she got there, we sat around to talk for a little bit. It was kind of awkward because we were strangers and we knew that we were about to be stuck together for a while. It became apparent fairly quick that we were going to get along just fine, though.

There was a bar right across the street so we decided to grab a beer and talk about what to do from here. We agreed to go venture out and go camping to see how things went before we actually started hiking a long distance.

I noticed that the North Fork American River was close by so we figured that would be our best bet for finding a spot to camp around here. We took some side roads and came to a dead end at someone's house. There was a lady outside and we asked if we could make our way through her property to get down to the river. She was fine with it.

When we got there, we put my tent up and left our gear so we could go hiking. We ended up having a blast, walking along the river and just being silly. I decided to jump into the river to see what she would do. I needed someone who was a little wild if they were going to be hanging around. She jumped in too so I knew she would be a good companion for me. Nature boy and nature girl. This should go well!

She was the first person to ever camp with me, though. I didn't know how this was going to go. I didn't want her to feel uncomfortable about sleeping in the tent with me so I didn't put my gear in until she had settled in first. She asked, "Do you still have enough room?"

She was a petite girl so I kind of laughed and said "Yeah, I think I can make that work."

It wasn't awkward at all. What a relief that was. I was kind of prepared for her to kick me out of my house but this was much better.

I must have made her feel pretty comfortable because when we woke up we were cuddling. I hadn't felt that in a while. It was really nice. We're going to be hiking buddies and cuddle buddies? This is going to be great!

I had been alone for so long and having her company made me feel not so wild. She brought me back to reality in a sense. I had grown a bit weary and cold towards people. It was nice to have someone to share this with.

We packed up and made our way back into town to grab some coffee when we ran into this guy named Ben. He talked to us for a while and offered us to come hang out at his place in Sacramento.

Megan was living in Auburn so we figured we could hike back to her place after spending the night with Ben. A good 20-mile hike would be enough to see how well we hiked together. We made it back to Auburn the next day and instead of going straight to her house, we decided to go back down to the river to camp for another night.

We talked about us becoming a couple and I thought it sounded like a good idea. We both seemed to be on the same page, we were getting along great, we were going to be together for a while, and we were both single. So why not?

We camped next to the river again that night and then in the morning we made our way to her house. She was living with her grandparents at the time and she wanted them to meet me.

When we got there here grandparents both took a liking to me really quick. It was nice. They liked me. I liked them. I was dating their granddaughter and they approved of me. I couldn't have asked for anything better.

Megan had some things to take care of before she could take off hiking so I went ahead and called Rob. I told him to go ahead and get his bus ticket for Sacramento and I'd be there when he got there. He said he would be there in three days. Perfect timing. I wanted to get into Sacramento and scope everything out so I could find out where we should and shouldn't go.

I would stay the night with Megan and then I'd head off to Sacramento in the morning. Her grandparents said "Hey, when your brother gets home I need you guys to go pick up a few things from the grocery store."

When her brother got there, he asked me if I wanted to smoke. I have smoked a few times in the past so I wasn't against it. I figured it would kind of help us bond a little bit. I was dating his sister after all.

He handed it to me first and I smoked it like you would normally smoke, well, marijuana. Then he looked at me with huge eyes and said, "Damn, dude. You must dab a lot, huh?"

I replied, "What? What's that?" He started laughing and asked if I was serious. I had never heard of "dabs" before. He said, "It's basically concentrated marijuana. I've never seen someone hit it like that." I was thinking, "Oh, crap. Well, too late now." I didn't feel anything, though, so I figured it must not be so bad.

Megan came in and said to her brother, "Hey, don't smoke. Grandma needs us to run to the store to pick up some groceries." I wasn't going to ride with someone under the influence, he hadn't smoked, and I still felt fine. So, we made our way to the store.

As soon as we walked into the store it hit me. Everything appeared to be shrinking and growing and I found everything to be the most hysterical thing in the world. I was trying to keep my composure, though. I did pretty well up until we were heading for the check-out. That's when it really hit me and it was like time had nearly come to a complete stop, but I was still functioning in normal time.

I heard Megan say "Hey, Jake, can you grab that pie." I looked down at it and for whatever reason I decided to show off my time-altering skills.

I karate chopped the pie off of the table it was sitting on, saw a lady scream, stared her directly in the eyes, spun around, and caught the pie in one hand just before it hit the floor. I never even took my eyes off of the lady that was screaming. She wasn't actually screaming, though. That's impossible. It happened too fast for her to scream but to me it looked like she was screaming because time had slowed down so much.

I turned to hand Megan the pie and she had the craziest look on her face. The kind of look you would have if you had just witnessed some sort of miracle. Then just as fast as it happened it was over with. I still felt a little weird but at least that whole "speeding through time" feeling was gone.

We made it back to the house and everything began to sound weird. Man, I was really tripping. Everything sounded huge, deep, and drawn out. I couldn't listen to people talk without laughing but I was trying to hide it so hard. I went to the bathroom so I could try to get myself together. I didn't want her grandparents knowing that I was as high as a kite. I just thought I was smoking a little pot, man. I didn't even want to get high. I just wanted to feel, you know, a little high. Not like this!

Megan knocks on the door and says, "Hey, are you alright? Dinner is ready." I said, "Yeah. I think so. I just needed a minute for that stuff to wear off. Let's go eat."

So, I'm sitting at the table and I quickly realize that it most certainly has not worn off. Everyone's voice still sounded the same and I put my head down so they wouldn't see me laughing.

Everyone thought that I was praying before our meal, which made it worse. I couldn't stop laughing. I wasn't laughing out loud but I was on the verge of it. I had tears rolling down my cheeks, though.

And then I hear Megan's grandma whisper to her, "Does he always pray this long?" Oh, my god, I am about to lose it and everyone is going to know that I am stoned out of my mind. I look up with the biggest grin on my face and said, "Alright. Let's eat!"; as if I was in charge of the dinner situation or something?

It worked at least but I became convinced that everyone knew that I was blitzed, which made it easier for me to relax. After we finished eating Megan's grandma leans over me and says, "Would you like anymore food?" and a huge wave hit me when she did that. It was like her voice shook my entire body.

I said "No. I'm good. Thanks, though." Apparently, after that, according to Megan, I stood there staring at their microwave for about an hour, and then I turned to say, "You guys have a nice microwave." Then I was completely sober. I haven't smoked anything since!

The next morning, I left Megan's house and headed back for Sacramento. I tried to find a good spot to camp that was somewhat close to the bus station so Rob and me wouldn't have to walk too far when he got there.

Pretty much everywhere that I thought to look was already taken by homeless people. That's something that I actually got really good at, finding homeless people. Eventually, I got to where I could just look at a spot and tell exactly where they were. If there was ever a job to find these people then I'd be set for life. Who was I to say anything, though? I was homeless. I guess we all kind of think the same when it comes to urban camping.

I ended up finding a spot that seemed relatively safe. Someone had been here before but I could tell it had been deserted a long time ago. I'd camp here tonight and see if I have any bad experience before I bring Rob into it.

The night went on without any disturbances so I waited around until Rob's bus came in. He finally got there around 2:00 a.m. and I immediately got him to follow me down to our spot for the night.

While we were walking I noticed that he had a school backpacked and I said "Oh, man, that's not gonna work. It'll do for a couple of days but don't worry. I'll find a way to get you all hooked up."

That night was pretty funny. Rob was already getting spooked out by everything and then I asked him to show me what all he had brought in his backpack that he was calling a "book bag". "First thing, man. We call these packs. Ha! Don't ever call my pack a book bag."

He empties out his pack and I start tossing out the things he wouldn't need. He had way too many clothes. At least get rid of all those socks and toilet paper. I showed him my gear to give him a good idea of what he would need and let him decide on what he wanted to carry, but I gave   some   suggestions.

6

I gave him a list of things before he came but he must have thought I was under prepared. It's common for new hikers to start out with too much stuff. His gear was just ridiculously funny, though. At least we laughed about it instead of making it some huge deal. We would get him squared away.

Later on, I hear him snacking on something and I told him there's no food in the tent. I look over and he has a huge bag of tortilla shells. This was too funny but I made him go put it in my food bag that I had hanging up in a tree nearby. I'm sure there weren't any bears in the area but it was something that I had gotten used to doing every night and needed to get him into the habit. I told him to get some sleep because I get up early. This was going to feel like boot camp for him.

I woke up before Rob and had everything packed up and ready to go, except for my tent because he was inside of it. I even took the poles out. The mesh part of my tent was just lying over him. I sat there to keep a lookout and let him wake up on his own.

When he woke up he started freaking out because everything was gone and the tent was just lying down on top of him. "I was wondering when you were gonna wake up!" He thought I had done up and left him there. Ha!

I knew he would catch on eventually so I didn't pressure him or anything. He wasn't used to this lifestyle. I'm not even sure if he had ever even been camping, so I gave him some props for even wanting to give this a try.

We went into town so we could get some coffee. I said, "Let me show you how to get coffee." I pointed down at the ground and there was a penny. I said, "Any time you see change you pick up. We'll have enough for coffee when we make it to the store."

He was having a hard time finding any change but I had been doing this for so long that I could spot a penny from 20 feet away. Not just pennies but all sorts of change.

When we got to the store I said, "Show me what you got". He had about eleven cents. I laughed and pulled out about $6 worth. He was really shocked but I was used to it. It had pretty much become my hobby to pick up change as I was walking.

I went into the store to store to get us some energy drinks instead of coffee, since that was more what he was into. I didn't mind. But when I came back out he was holding a large bag. I asked him what was inside and he said some lady just stopped to give it to him. It was full of food. I patted him on the back and said, "There you go. Now you're officially a bum!" It was some really good food, too!

She also gave him $20 and he asked me if I wanted to split it. I told him to hang onto it. I'd received a few care packages from my followers and saved most of the money so I wasn't doing too bad. I tried to use as little money as possible and most of the time people offered to help. We needed to save our money for things like gear. The rest would pretty much fall into place. We did go get a couple of beers to celebrate his arrival, though. One for me and one for him.

After that, I got a call from Megan. She said she was

behind on everything but she would catch up with us later, so me and Rob would continue on from there. We walked around Sacramento for most of the day just checking everything out, and then as the day came to an end we made our way to the river on the northwest side of town. We ended up sleeping at a park, just laid on the ground.

Rob actually woke up before me and said "Dude? Did it rain last night? Everything is soaking wet." I laughed at him and said, "No, dude. That's condensation. It's good for you. You ready to start walk?"

We looked at my GPS and I asked him if he thought he could make it to Woodland. It was only about 20 miles. That's nothing for me but I knew it would be pretty tough for a new guy, especially Rob since he was a little on the big size.

He had to stop and take a lot of breaks but we made it before dark so I was actually really proud of him. He had gotten his new blisters already and everything. When we made it into the city limits we decided to stop and this Mexican Restaurant. I didn't want to shove him straight into dumpster diving yet. I wanted to kind of ease him into it and I felt like he deserved it.

While we were eating our dinner, this guy comes to sit with us and hears about how I've come across the country. He asks if we'd mind him buying us a few beers at the bar right across the street. We took him up on his offer. When we were sitting there having drinks this lady sits beside me and says "So, you just walked across the country, huh?" Her name was Christy and she had a few drinks with me and then said that me and Rob could crash at her house tonight. Really? That's awesome!

She offered to let us stay with her for a few days so she could give us a good time in Woodland. Our first day she took us to meet her friend who lived in a shop. He was an artist and made all kinds of neat things. It looked like a museum in there. He was a really nice guy and got a kick out of Rob. Rob was an aspiring comedian so he could entertain anyone with a sense of humor. I was more of the rugged wild man. We made for an interesting pair to be hiking together.

After that she took us to back to a restaurant that she owned and let us have whatever we wanted. She kind of made it known to everyone who we were and what I had just accomplished. People were really excited and getting pictures with us. It was really fun. I don't know what happened to Rob because I found myself surrounded by a lot of women. I knew he was around here somewhere, though.

We go back to her place after closing and get some rest. She said tomorrow she would be taking us wake boarding. I'd never been wake boarding before but I grew up skateboarding. How hard could it be?

When we get to the wake boarding park Rob decides to just hang around. He didn't really feel up to it. The owners made me sign a waiver and told me to have at it. Free of charge. I walked out like a professional but it took me almost all day just to be able to make one full run. It was fun, though!

Christy had some work to do at the restaurant but told me to give her a call when we were finished and she would come back to pick us up. Since I was already pretty sore and I could tell that Rob was starting to get bored, I got out of there and called Christy up.

We went back to her restaurant for dinner and then we headed back to her house. She asked if we'd like to check out some vineyards tomorrow. She got the wine for her restaurant from them so she could go out any time she wanted. I thought that sounded cool. I'd never been to a vineyard before.

When we got there, they were wine tasting and handed me and Rob glass after glass. I'm not really sure about wine tasting but I know how to drink. Me and Rob ended up getting pretty silly. The vineyard owners didn't seem to mind. I think they were all feeling kind of funny.

Then we went back to Christy's restaurant for some more drinking. Again, I ended up getting swamped by the ladies and lose track of Rob. I felt kind responsible for him but I knew he could take care of himself.

Tomorrow we were going to have to work off all of our partying, though. They have this festival once a month (this was April 11, 2015 by the way) and Christy would need our help with setting everything up and then cleaning up after. She deserved a lot more than that but it was her call. We we're happy to help!

The next day me and Rob were making our way for the coast. We still had a pretty good way to go. I was a little worried about Rob making it but at least we had picked him up a new pack, some better shoes, trekking poles, mole skin for his feet, and a tarp. I told him that he was welcome to bunk with me but he would need that tarp once Megan reunited with us. I taught him how to properly set his tarp up to use as a shelter but he preferred to just roll up in it like a burrito. Whatever works for you, man!

We made it about 20 miles from Woodland before it got dark and we camped just right off from the road. Rob was still kind of spooked and kept asking me if there were bears out there. How was I supposed to know? I couldn't offer much comfort because I didn't want to say there wasn't and then a bear come up wandering up to us.

The next morning, we were making our way for Guinda. I ended up getting stopped by the cops because I had my machete strapped to the side of my pack. They kept calling my knives weapons and I told them they weren't weapons. They were tools. I never used my knives as weapons so I wasn't lying. They were really skeptical up until I ended up mentioning that we had just left Christy's back in Woodland. They knew her and decided we checked out. We ended up bringing Christy's name up quite a few times. She was pretty popular around these parts.

Jody had found out that we were heading into Guinda and had sent us out a care package. Jody sent me so many care packages in case you haven't noticed that yet. You'll probably hear me bring that up several more times.

Since the package wasn't going to be there for a few days we decided to make it a slow day. It wasn't even that far of a walk, anyways. Maybe 10 miles from where we were at. So, yeah, these next few days were going to be lazy. I didn't mind, though. I had a stress fracture in my hip and I could really use the break. I wouldn't have taken it otherwise.

When we got close to town we noticed there was a park that went down to a river. We walked down there and decided that we would camp here for the night. I knew there was a store just up the road so I went to check it out while Rob hung out down by the creek.

I walk into this restaurant and they automatically noticed that I was a traveler. They asked if I needed anything to eat. I said that sounded great but I had a buddy with me down at the river. I just wanted to see what our options were in case we needed something. They told me to get him and come back later for dinner.

I went back to tell Rob the good news. He was stoked. Everything kept working out in our favor. We were both getting really lucky. He hadn't seen the harshness yet, but I was happy for the both of us.

We went swimming after I gave him the good news. We swam pretty much the whole day. I figured now would be a good time to teach Rob how to fish. He started looking for a stick to use as a fishing pole and I said, "No. Not like that." I walked into the water and stood there with me hands in the water for a few minutes. He said, "No way are you going to catch a.." I threw a fish at him and he freaked out. He got out there and tried it for a few minutes but decided that he'd rather skip rocks. I can get in on that, too.

It was starting to get late so we made our way up to the

restaurant. They told us to sit anywhere we like and asked us what we wanted. I said "We will take whatever you want to give us. We aren't picky." They ended up bringing us out two huge burgers and beers.

After we finished eating Rob asked the owner if he wanted us to do the dishes to pay for the meal and the owner said, "Fuck you!" He said it in a jokingly way, though. It was pretty funny. We thanked them and then made our way back down to the river to camp for the night.

The next morning, we sat around and pretty much did the same thing all day. Swimming and throwing rocks. When it started to get late we decided to head back up to the restaurant to grab us some dinner. This time I would insist on paying, though.

We ordered the same thing that they gave us the night before because it was pretty good. We ended up eating outside in the back and the cook, Jessie, came out with us. We sat around and talked for a little while and then he said "You guys don't have to worry about paying for that by the way. You can camp back here, too." These guys were awesome!

The next morning, we went to check and see if our package would arrive. We waited for the mail person, but when they got there, they said we didn't have a package. We went back over to the restaurant to just hang out in the back. They didn't mind. They even brought me out a guitar to help kill some time.

When Jessie got off of work he offered to let us come camp at his house. He used to be a traveler back before he settled down here in Guinda so he knew how it was.

We made us camp in his front yard because his wife wasn't comfortable with us being in the house but we didn't mind that. At least here we knew that we didn't have to about being caught for camping down at the river.

We had breakfast with Jessie and then went to check to see if the package had arrived yet. Still no dice. It should most certainly be here tomorrow, though. Jessie told us about this bridge right up the road from his house that we could camp under without any troubles. He said no one ever goes down there. So, we made our way down to our spot for the night.

This part of the river seemed like it would be a much better spot than the other place we had been going to. We swam pretty much all day. That's all we really had to do. We swam until it got dark and then turned in early. It was so early that Rob even decided to take a couple of my sleeping pills. I had bouts of insomnia so I carried them with me in case I missed a couple of nights.

It was around 2:00 a.m. or so when I heard a loud splash in the water. It sounded like someone threw a large boulder over the side of the bridge. I began to listen to see if I heard anyone but I never did, so I tried to go back to sleep.

Then I heard it again. I stuck my head out and turned on my headlamp. I sat there for a few minutes to wait and see if I saw anything. I turned my headlamp off. About ten seconds later I heard it again and it sounded like it was right beside the tent. I turned my headlamp on but there weren't any ripples in the water or anything.

I woke Rob up and told him there was some weird shit going on. I told him to listen. Then it sounded like boulders were dropping from up the river and making their way down. We must have heard it about ten times or so and it kept getting closer. The last one hit right in front of us and made a huge splash.

We were both really freaked out now. I was more concerned than Rob, though. He was kind of loopy from those sleeping pills and said it was probably a fish. I was wide awake dealing with this pretty much by myself. I wanted to get up and get out of there. I opened my tent door all the way because I wanted to get out and figure out what exactly was going on.

As soon as I started to get out of my tent these rocks

started flying around everywhere. I know it sounds crazy but there were probably, I don't know, maybe a hundred rocks just flying all over the place. They were hitting the tent, the wall behind us, and smashing into the water.

Rob was awake now! We were both freaking out! We wanted to get up and leave but we were scared that we would get hit by all of these rocks that were flying around. We put our gear over our heads just in case one came flying in and hit us.

After about ten minutes of this it had finally stopped. I stuck my head out to see if the bridge had fallen apart. The bridge looked fine. This didn't make any sense. I laid there until the sun came up, just listening for anything else. Rob was able to get some sleep after that, though. I have no idea how. Those sleeping pills must have done a number one him. I would need a whole bottle to even make me feel the least bit tired.

Even though Rob was able to get some sleep he was still freaked out about what had happened. We were packing up to get the heck out of there. While we were packing everything up, I noticed a man on the other side of the river. He was walking around with a fishing pole so I didn't think anything about it.

I continued packing my things and once I had my pack on I turned back around and the man was gone. Me and Rob both saw him but neither of us saw him leave. Man, this place is creepy. We got out of there!

While we were leaving we kept looking around for the guy that we thought was fishing. We never saw him again, though. We couldn't even figure out how he would have gotten over there without walking through the river. There weren't any trails that went to that side. I was awake all night and I never heard anything walking through the brush. No one could walk through there without making noise.

We went straight back to Jessie's house to ask him if he had ever had any weird experiences while camping down there. He said "Oh, I've never gone camping down there. I've been swimming down there a few times, though."

We told him about what had happened and he said, "Well, it could be haunted. There's an old story about a lady that claimed she met the devil down at the river." Me and Rob agreed that we would never go back down there again!

Jessie gave us a ride back down to the post office since he had to go back that way to go to work anyways. Thank goodness, our package had finally arrived. We didn't feel like hanging around here anymore.

Jody sent enough food and cash for me and Rob to make it for quite a while. It added some weight that Rob wasn't used to but I told him he would get used to it. My pack was around 70lbs and his was around 35lbs. He didn't want to complain too much because he knew I'd make him carry mine if he did. Ha!

We made our way from here to Clearlake Oaks. We made it about 30 miles or so before we sat up camp. That would leave only 10 miles into Clearlake Oaks, which would be a good start for the day.

It seemed kind of like a rough neighborhood so went didn't hang around for too long. We just needed to fill up on water and then we were on our way. After we got out of the city, it was nice walking around the lake; but the roads were windy and there was no shoulder.

Rob was really nervous about it but there wasn't any other option. It slowed us down quite a bit, having to continuously stop and try to get out of the way of traffic. One side of the road was a steep incline and the other side was a steep drop down into the rocks and water below.

Once we were finally to the top of the cliff we noticed an RV camp. We asked the owner how much it would cost for us to pitch our tent here and he told us it would be $50. Okay, scratch that idea. We continued walking until we found a building that looked abandoned and decided to camp behind it for free.

By the next afternoon we had made it into Calpella when we realized that the highway had turned into an interstate. Since you can walk on the interstate we decided to try and hitch hike up to Willits. I was really against it but there was no other way.

We tried hitch hiking for about two hours or so when we decided to walk into town. Maybe we would have better luck asking for a ride at a gas station.

When we got into town we noticed that there was a bus that ran from here to Willits and it would only cost us about two dollars each so we agreed to do that instead of bothering people. We made it just in time to catch the bus. We were sitting there for just a few minutes before it arrived.

Willits was different from any other city I had ever been to. I don't know if I mean that in a good way or a bad way. I saw a lot of people walking around drinking beer. I saw a man punch a woman and then the cops asked me and Rob what happened.

Then me and Rob took turns going into this store to fill up on water. We had to take turns because you aren't allowed to bring backpacks in and there was absolutely no way that we would leave our things unattended here.

While I was in the store I heard a customer asking one of the cashiers if she knew where he could get some cocaine. They weren't being quiet about it either. There were people standing all around and no one seemed to find this conversation odd except for me.

I came back outside and let Rob go in to fill his water up. While I was outside waiting for him some guy kept trying to get me to come behind the store with him.

This place was making me uncomfortable. We definitely have to make it out of here before tonight. When Rob came out we looked at my map and agreed to take a bus until the next stop towards Ft. Bragg. That would get us out of here and then we could hike the rest of the way to the coast. This place was just too sketchy and if we didn't take a bus we wouldn't make it out of here before dark.

We'd still get to hike through the Jackson State Forest but not have to worry about all these people. So, we hopped onto the bus and waited for the next stop. I don't remember where it dropped us off at but it was a very small town. I don't think it even had a gas station. It had a school, though, and some kind of factory. That was about it. We could find a place to camp here. No problem!

It took us a couple of days to get into Ft. Bragg, California. Rob was happy to see the ocean but it was a greater feeling for me. I had finally made it across the country. It took me six months and twenty-two days. Not too bad!

That was something Rob couldn't understand but I had to walk in to get my feet wet. Now that I had made it across the United States it was time to begin my journey to Alaska.

Megan ended up calling and said she would be able to get a Greyhound Bus to Ukiah but didn't know how she would make up to Ft. Bragg. I told her that I would take a local bus to come down and meet up with her when she got there. She said she would be there in two days. That gave me and Rob time to hang out in Ft. Bragg.

Ft. Bragg was pretty laid back. I wouldn't have any problems hanging around here. We needed to scope out a good place to claim as our home base for a few days, though.

We ended up walking towards the north side of town, walked along a trail, and found a large tree that thick brush and branches hanging down. There was just enough room underneath all of the limbs for my tent to fit. You couldn't see it from the trail and we had a perfect view of the ocean from here. This would be a great spot. Now, what to do with the rest of our time?

We still had plenty of daylight left so we walked up to a gas station and took us a six pack down to the beach.

There weren't any other people around. It was just me and Rob hanging out and enjoying the fruits of our labor.

It started to get late so we headed back to our camp. We had a perfect view of a sunset and joked about how writers could come here and make a book about.

"The view was inspirational so I felt inspired to write an inspirational book about feeling inspired by all of this inspiration."

Which is kind of funny considering that I have ended up writing a book about. Not exactly in those words but you get the idea. There was no doubt, though, if you weren't feeling inspired this was the right place to get it.

The next morning, we found a homeless shelter. We were both ready for a shower. They even let us do our laundry there and told us that we could get some food just up the road.

I still had a lot of food from the package Jody had sent but Rob wanted to go so I walked with him. It was kind of like a grocery store. They gave Rob a shopping cart and let him walk around and pick out whatever he wanted. He got more than we could pack so we hung around and handed some of it out to people who looked like they could use it.

After that we decided to head down to Glass Beach. I didn't know what to expect but the name was very fitting. Glass from the ocean had washed up here. The entire beach was covered in glass but they weren't sharp. The water had smoothed the pieces out so you could just walk around on them barefoot, and it actually felt really nice on your feet. The pieces were all different colors, shapes, and sizes.

I decided to open up a pack of crackers and several ground squirrels came down out of the rocks to investigate. I tossed out a few crumbs and all of a sudden, we were surrounded by these squirrels.

They would eat right out of our hand. They weren't nervous at all. I even got to pet one of them. This was all fun and everything but I needed to get down to Ukiah so I could meet up with Megan.

I asked Rob if he wanted to come with me or if he just wanted to hang out here. He said that he would just hang around. Then I headed up to catch my bus. I'd be there a few hours before Megan got there but I was fine with that.

I went down to the Greyhound Bus stop and played my harmonica while I was waiting. I wasn't panhandling but I ended up making about $10. I was just trying to pass the time but if people liked what they heard then, yeah, I didn't mind.

When Megan got there, we went back to the local bus stop to catch our ride up to Ft. Bragg. We made it back before it got dark so that gave her and Rob time to get acquainted. They seemed to get along pretty well so no worries there.

I took Megan down to where we had been camping and she loved it. It really was the perfect spot. We all sat out and watched the sunset until it was time to turn in for the night.

Me and Megan were in the tent and Rob was just in front of us rolled up in his tarp. I felt kind of bad for him but he wasn't interested in setting it up like a shelter. He didn't mind his "burrito method". If he was fine with it then I was fine with it.

The next morning, we were going to start heading up the coast but we stopped to get some breakfast first.

We ended up running into these ladies from Sweden. They were planning on hiking the Pacific Crest Trail and said that we could come and hang out with them at their beach house if we wanted to. Me and Megan decided to go along with them but Rob decided to stay back at the beach.

When we got to their house we sat around and talked about hiking gear mostly. They wanted to hear about what it was like backpacking in America but I wanted to know what it was like backpacking in Sweden. We shared some stories back and forth until it was time to go to bed. Me and Megan even got one of their spare rooms to ourselves. Home away from home! They give us a ride back to the beach after we have breakfast and we meet back up with Rob. We decided to go back down to the homeless shelter so we could all get a shower.

After that we hung around at the beach all day again. It was starting to get late and it looked like we would be spending one more night in Ft. Bragg. I was fine with that but I was ready to get moving. My time to make it through Canada was wearing thinner with each passing day.

Megan said if we wanted to go to the bar to get a few drinks she would pay for it. So, that's what we did. We hadn't been to any bars here and I was always interested in trying new beers. I knew they brewed their own stouts here and I was always down to try a new dark beer. After we had a few drinks we decided to do some night walking to make it at least a little farther from where we had been. I was ready to put some miles down.

It was about midnight or so when I heard Rob and Megan outside of the tent, talking and laughing. I got up to see what was going on. While I was passed out they decided to go back to the bar and have a few more drinks. Megan crawled into my tent and then I went back to sleep.

When I woke up I noticed that everything in my pack and been pulled out and scattered all over the place. I noticed that my medication was missing. It was a scheduled drug that I was prescribed for my PTSD and I knew that Rob used to have a drug and stealing problem.

I woke Rob up and asked him if had gotten into my pack last night after they got back from drinking. He yelled at me and said "Dude, don't ever wake me up and ask me shit like that."

I replied, "Well, all of my stuff is scattered everywhere and some of my pills are missing."

Then we kind of got into it and Megan woke up. She was telling me to calm down because Rob hadn't been in my pack. I got mad at her for taking his side. She didn't know what had happened. She was in the tent sleeping with me. Why was she taking his side?

I never had any proof that he took my medication but I couldn't be with them if I didn't trust them anymore. So, I told them good luck and that I had to travel on by myself.

I felt bad for leaving them but I also felt betrayed. I knew that together they would fine. I later heard that Megan went back home and Rob took a bus up to Portland, Oregon and found a job at a head shop. I was at ease knowing that Megan had made it home and Rob was out doing his own thing.

It was about 60 miles to Garberville and I felt like I could make that before it got dark so I got to stepping. It was a nice walk going up highway 1 through the Redwood forest. I saw a few black bears, too. They all ran off as soon as they saw me but I felt like I was back where I belonged.

The hike seemed a little dangerous because there was barely any shoulder and lots of curves. The trees were right on the shoulder, too, which created terrible blind spots. I had to stand behind a tree several times and wait until I felt like it was safe to run around it. I had a lot of close calls doing that. I had to walk into the road, though.

The other side of the trees was a steep hill and you couldn't get around the trees on that side. Honestly, I don't recommend anyone attempt to hike up this highway. There were some great sights along the way but the traffic made it feel like a death trap.

While I was walking up the highway I came across this place that had a lot of neat wood carvings sitting outside. There was one of Shrek, Pinocchio, Bigfoot, and a few others.

Not far from that was a house that was built into a tree. That will give you an idea of just how large these trees actually are! I think the house in the tree had even been on "Ripley's Believe it or Not". I never looked into that but I'm pretty sure I remember seeing a sign that said so.

I also passed by a tree that had been given the name "Grandfather Tree". It was 1,800 years old, stood at 265 feet, and had a diameter of 24 feet. I took a picture of it but the picture did it no justice. It just looked like any other tree from the photo. I guess that's just something you would just have to see for yourself.

I was just outside of Garberville when I came across a gas station where I could fill up on water. I noticed a man sitting in a lawn chair next to the building just across from the gas station. He seemed really interesting so I walked over to talk to him.

He was an older man. Probably in his late 50s. He was sporting a long white beard, a purple and yellow striped jacket, camouflage pants, some old beat up boots, and a mountain bike with a huge trailer on the back of it.

I asked him what he was up to and he said he was just taking a break from work. I asked him what he did for work. He said he washed people's windows as they were leaving the gas station. He had it set up right. The gas station had a "No Loitering" sign but he wasn't at the gas station. He was sitting in front of an old abandoned store just across from it.

He asked where I was heading and I told him I was heading up to Alaska. He said, "Oh, there's probably a lot of bears up there. What you got there? Is that some of that bear spray? I'll show you what I got."

He pulls out a laser pointer and said when he comes across the bears around here he just shines the light into their eyes and they hated it. He said, "The same bear comes down to the river over there every morning. I shined this light in his eyes one time and he hasn't ever approached me since." I found him to be interesting enough that I asked if I could take his picture. He didn't mind.

As I was making my way into Garberville I was stopped by two officers. They said that I couldn't be walking out here. I tried telling them that I was walking across America for mental health awareness and I understood the risks. They said that what I was doing was noble but they'd have to give me ride into Garberville. They gave me the money to catch a bus to Eureka and said if they saw me back out on the highway they would have to take me to jail, give me a fine, and confiscate all of my weapons. I decided that taking the bus sounded like a better option.

I get into Eureka and realize that I have to poop. I couldn't find anywhere that would let me use their restroom. I couldn't even go into a gas station. I tried to go into one gas station and they said "Sorry. Our bathrooms are for customers only." I threw a sucker on the counter and said, "Okay. Here. Ring this up." The cashier looked at me and said, "No, sir. You're just trying to use the restroom." I said, "Okay."

I walked across the street and pooped behind a bush. I couldn't hold it anymore. I apologize for my indecency but I was turtling. I tried to use a restroom but no one would let me. I was behind a bush but it didn't offer very much protection. There were cars passing by and I could plainly see people's faces. I felt bad but relieved. That's what really matters, right? Jerks.

I already hated Eureka so I didn't stick around. Not that I needed to anyways. If I wanted to get through Canada before the weather turned bad I was going to have to keep a fifty mile per day pace. So, I pushed on into McKinleyville.

I had heard a lot of good things about Eureka but McKinleyville was more my style. Everyone seemed to be easier going. Maybe I had just run into the wrong people back in Eureka but it left a sour taste.

I walked down to the end of one of the streets so I could try to find a nice spot to camp next to the ocean. It sounds like an easy task but a lot of the places were either fenced off, the woods were too thick, or there was just a straight drop into some rocks.

I found a trail and decided to take it. It ran along the beach so I was sure that it would lead me to a good spot eventually. I walked for about five miles before gaining access to the beach but it was totally worth it. I couldn't see a sign of anyone in either direction. Just the way I liked it!

That night, while I was lying in my tent, my mom called and asked if I would come home for Mother's Day if she paid for me a bus ticket. She knew I was heading for Alaska with intentions on staying so I couldn't say no. So, the next day I headed back down to Arcata and hopped on my bus to Tennessee. Oh, moms!

I made it into Tennessee the day before Mother's Day, May 10, 2015. My mom picked me up at the bus station and then we went out to eat. She talked about how much I had changed. That much time on the road will do that to you. I went from looking like civilized human being to something you'd see on the Discovery Channel. I felt great, though!

A few days had passed and I started to feel like maybe I should just stick around here. I had made my way across the country. Could I accept that? Was that enough? I figured I would try to settle down and see how things went.

I started working some odd jobs and began saving for a car. I was trying to fight my urges to leave but after a month I just couldn't take it anymore. It was too late to walk through Canada so what was I going to do? I came up with two options: I can either keep saving up for a car and drive to Alaska, or I can take a plane. I didn't feel like waiting anymore so I went with my second choice.

I did some time/money management and realized that I could fly from Nashville, Tennessee to San Diego, California. Then I could walk from San Diego up to San Francisco to fly up to Anchorage, Alaska. I paid for my ticket from San Francisco to Anchorage well in advance and it was only $150. The only catch was that I would have to walk from San Diego to San Francisco within 30 days. I think I can manage that!

Another catch was that I had to be in Nashville, Tennessee in order to catch my flight to San Diego, California. I gave myself a week to make it. I figured I could make it in a few days if I hitch hiked. I ended up getting a ride from Bradford, Tennessee to Jackson. Then I ran into my old friend Sydney! Her and her boyfriend said I could stay with them in Memphis and then they would bring me back to Nashville.

I spent the night with them and they ended up getting drunk, and disappearing. When morning came I couldn't find them anywhere. I couldn't get in contact with them. I was stuck in Memphis and I needed to be getting to Nashville.

I hung out around the interstate all day, trying to hitch a ride, but no one ever stopped. It was about 4:00 p.m. and I began to feel the effects of heat exhaustion. I went to lie down in the shade and I passed out.

I woke around 10:00 p.m. and I had a terrible headache. I also had blood on my sleeping pad. I assume that it came from my nose but I wasn't sure. I sat up and drank about two liters of water and went back to sleep. The next morning, I make my way to a gas station when a police officer decides to stop and talk to me. I told him the situation and he offered to buy me breakfast.

A few hours later I get a message from Sydney's grandma. She apologized about how Sydney had disappeared on me and offered to buy me a bus ticket to Nashville. She didn't have to do this but I was so thankful! I made my way straight to the bus station and I was on my way to Nashville.

When I made it to Nashville I still had two days before I had to catch my plane. Luckily, this lady I went to school with, Samantha, had moved to Nashville a few years ago, and said I could stay with her.

The first night after I got there I just got a shower, did

some laundry (my clothes were all crusted over from sweat), and I went to sleep. The next day, me and her husband went to the bar to grab a few drinks.

After we left the bar we went back to the house and had dinner and then I went straight to bed. I was really tired and I was assuming that I probably had a heat stroke that night back in Memphis. I just felt kind of off. I've been through it before, though. I knew my body would bounce back.

The next morning, they gave me a ride to the airport. Flying with a couple of large knives will make you feel super sketchy. They were in my pack, which was going into cargo, but you never know what to expect with airline security these days.

After we landed in San Diego I opened up my pack to make sure everything was fine. Inside I found a letter of inspection due to dangerous items. At least they didn't take anything or make a scene out of it.

Once I was in San Diego I decided to make the most of my time. I knew that all I had to do to make it to San Francisco within 30 days was to walk at least 18 miles per day. I could easily pull 50 mile days so I could take a couple of days off here and there. I just had to make sure that I kept up with my miles and my days so I didn't get too far behind.

I made my way to coast and walked along the sidewalk, checking out all of the boats; just enjoying the day. I got a message from a girl who had been following my page. She knew that I was in San Diego and asked if I wanted to hang out. I said "Yeah, sure." So, she came to pick me up.

She lived about 40 miles from the coast. I didn't know how to feel about this but she seemed like a nice person. We get back to her apartment and her roommate says that I have to leave. That I made her feel uncomfortable. This girl that just picked me up says, "I'm sorry but you have to go."

She didn't offer to give me a ride back or anything. I

ended up having to walk back to San Diego, which kind of sucked, but it wasn't like I wasn't used to walking or anything.

I get back into San Diego after dark and try to find a place to sleep. I wasn't having very good luck. It was just too crowded of a city and I didn't have the time to inspect the area yet. I spent hours looking for a spot and ended up sleeping behind an air conditioning unit. Not much coverage but it would have to do.

The next morning, I decide to make my way down to the beach. Alone my way I saw several signs but two of them really stood out to me, personally. One of the signs read, "CATERPILLAR SHEDS IT'S SKIN TO FIND A BUTTERFLY WITHIN" and the other was "SLOW DOWN AND TAKE IT EASY BABY". I could definitely relate to both of these signs.

Once I made it down to the beach I walked down to the water and I somehow felt bored of it. I guess because I had no one to enjoy it with. I don't know. The beach was divided into two sides. One side was for people and the other side was for people with their dogs. I didn't have a dog but I went over to that side. I'd rather sit and watch dogs than people.

After watching people play with their dogs for about an hour or so I decided to follow this trail that went back inland. I noticed a couple of older hippies sitting around and they asked what I was up to so I went and hung out with them for a while.

Once it got dark they got into their van and took off. I decided to just make my way over to this tree and threw my sleeping bag down on the dirt and called it a night.

The next morning, I decided to head up to the zoo but when I got there they said that I couldn't go in with my pack. I asked if they would mind hanging onto it for me but they said they couldn't for liability reasons.

I made my way back down towards the beach and made friends with some beach bums. They were sitting around telling jokes for twenty-five cents. The girl that was telling the jokes actually had a lot of good jokes. I was impressed. I've never met anyone who knew so many. She never used the same joke twice, either. After they had enough money saved up they left to go buy some liquor. I wasn't in the mood for all of that so I parted ways with them.

Then one of my blog followers sent me a message and asked if I'd like to come stay with them for a few days. I took them up on that offer. Jim and Shany were their names. Jim came to pick me after he got off of work and then we headed back to their place.

While I was staying with them I ended up purchasing a bus ticket up to Long Beach. It was only like $40 so I didn't mind. I wasn't really too impressed with San Diego and from there up was mostly interstate.

They lived in an apartment that had a pool so I took it easy for a few days. Mostly drinking beer or swimming. Jim would come home from work and head up to his room while me and Shany stayed in the living room watching movies. She let me pick the movies that I wanted to watch. I hadn't watched any television in a long time so I was pretty bad at picking the movies. She teased me quite a bit about that.

I would be leaving tomorrow but today Jim and Shany were both off of work, so we went to one of the parks to walk around and enjoy the day. It was actually quite uneventful but we had a nice walk. It was the first day that I had been there that we all got to spend the whole day together.

When we got back to their apartment I checked my messages and noticed that I had received an email from Fox and Lionsgate asking me to send them in a video to participate in one of their survival shows. I didn't have any videos but I sent them in a lot of pictures that showed me doing some primitive hunting, making my own weapons, bow drill fires, trapping, building shelters, foraging, and all of that fun stuff. I never heard anything back from them, though. I guess they really did need a video. Oh, well..

7

The next morning, I was packed up and ready to go. My bus wasn't supposed to leave until around 9:00 a.m. but Jim had to be at work pretty early so we left around 6:00 a.m. or so.

After he dropped me off I quickly realized that this was not the bus station that I was supposed to be at. I looked at my GPS and noticed that it was about twenty miles away. I didn't mind walking but I wouldn't make it in time.

I called Jim to let him know that this was the wrong bus station. He apologized and said he needed to let his supervisor know what was going on and then he would head back to take me to the right bus station.

While I was sitting there waiting for him I noticed there was a homeless guy sleeping on the ground. This other homeless guy comes up and starts going through his things. I noticed that he took a bag of food from him. I didn't say anything because I didn't want to start any confrontation. After the thief left, I woke the man up to tell him what had happened.

Shany had sent me off with a few sandwiches so I gave them to him. A few other people were standing around and witnessed what happened, too. I was surprised that no one else cared to help this man out. He just had his food stolen and everyone just turned to look the other way. As is with those large cities I guess.

Anyways, Jim finally arrives and we throw my pack in his trunk. I apologized for the inconvenience but thanked him for coming back. He could have just left me out there but he was a good guy.

When I get to the right bus station I go up to show them my ticket and wait for my bus to arrive. It would take about an hour for it to get there so I pull my phone out and check up on my blog.

While I was on my phone I noticed this man walking around checking used needles to see if they had anything left in them. He saw me on my phone and thought that I was taking pictures of him. He started yelling at me and acting all kinds of crazy. I told him that I wasn't taking his picture but he needed to get out of my face. I was ready to throw down but he backed off.

I was of pretty good size at the time. I was probably more fit now than when I was in the military. Not only had I been cycling and carrying about 65 pounds on my back for nearly the past year, but I also did about three-hundred pushups every day (with my pack on).

I wasn't out there trying to look good or anything but when you're out there all alone you need to be able to take care of yourself. It was pretty hard for me to feel intimidated and I guess that junky could tell. I had been in similar situations and I knew what he was doing. I wasn't trying to cause any problems. Usually, the calmer you stay the wearier they become.

Finally! My bus had arrived and I was out of there! I didn't know what to expect from Santa Maria but I was ready for something new. I had a lot of fun hanging out with Shany and Jim but as for the rest of San Diego? Not one of my favorite cities.

Once I made it into Santa Maria I began to walk outside of the city limits to find a place to camp.

Tomorrow I would head back into town and see what I could get into. I made my way back into town and I already didn't like it here. Seemed to be a lot of gang activity in the area. I probably should have searched up the crime data report but I neglected to do so.

I found an empty parking lot and sat down to come up with some plans on where I should head to next. While I was sitting there I posted a picture on my blog and one of my followers happened to live here. He didn't message me but he recognized where I was at from the picture.

As I was sitting there a car pulls up and this man steps out, "Hey, Jake. I'm David. I've been following your travels and when you posted this picture I figured I'd swing by. I'm headed to work but I thought I'd stop by to give you something to drink and a few bucks." That was really unexpected!

I wandered around town for a while and started having bad panic attacks. I tried to make it back to where I had camped the night before but I just needed to get away from everyone.

I noticed this small alley between an old store and an auto shop so I squeezed back in there and slept off the rest of the day. That night got a little weird, though. People kept coming in and out of the auto shop. The alley I was in was just a few feet tall, enough for me to stay out of sight. If someone had peeked over for whatever reason then I would have been seen and who knows what would have happened in that case.

It was about 3:00 a.m. and I heard a few gun shots coming from the road behind me. This was working wonders for my PTSD. Okay, I'm out of here first thing in the morning. This isn't the place for me either. I went ahead and got a bus ticket for Santa Cruz.

Once I made it into Santa Cruz I could tell that I had made the right decision. There were still a lot of people but it had a much better vibe than San Diego and Santa Maria. I would also be able to take more time to enjoy myself and not be so stressed about making it to San Francisco on time. I had plenty of days left. Might as well "SLOW DOWN AND TAKE IT EASY BABY."

As soon as I get off of the bus I made my way to the beach. What else would you do if you were backpacking up the coast? So, anyways, I get down there and I see this strip that runs along the beach. There are several bars, restaurants, and a few small stores.

There were people all over the beach playing volleyball and just soaking up the sun. A real chill and laid-back kind of place, but with just the right amount of partying. Nothing too crazy.

So, I go into one of the bars to grab a few beers. Everyone's kind of looking at me funny because I look like a hobo. I mean I kind of was and kind of wasn't. I only flew a sign once. I never actually asked for help any other time. I had just been running into the right who wanted to help me along the way.

I pull out my wallet and hand the bartender my debit card, and everyone looks away. When you look the way I was looking, you kind of have to flaunt it that you got your financial situation under control or they will kick you out. It's just something that I picked up. Adapt and overcome.

I had maybe four beers and I was feeling pretty good. I wasn't drunk by any means but it was enough to calm my nerves. I was hoping to make some friends and I'm not really the best at starting conversations. At least with, you know, civilized people, people who were stuck in the system.

I could walk up to people who were like me with no problem, people who had my vibe. You learn how to pick up on that relatively quick when you're traveling. Especially, when you're doing it by yourself.

I go down to the beach and I put my pack where I can walk around without it, but still be able to keep an eye on it. I kept trying to talk to people but they just kept giving me nasty faces. I tried to find someone to hang out with for about three hours. It wasn't happening and it was a little depressing. At the time it was, anyways. I'm looking back at it now and laughing.

I gave up on making any friends and decided to wander off by myself. I walk along the beach for as long as I could (which wasn't very far) and there were these concrete columns to the foundation of a hotel. No one was over here so I decided to sit beside one of them.

I saw a sign that said there was no camping or sleeping on the beach, but no one was around so I figured that I would just sleep here. I didn't feel like wandering around after dark, hoping to find a good spot and not. So, I just threw my sleeping pad and sleeping bag down on the sand.

The next day when I woke up there were life guards in training, doing exercises on the beach. Coming from the military, it was pretty funny watching them struggle to do these exercises. If my captain had our platoon doing something this easy we would have thought something was wrong with him.

After I had my laugh, I got up and walked back up to the main strip. I wanted to grab some coffee and then go walk out onto the pier. When I got to the end of the pier I heard a sea lion barking. I looked over the edge and there were about six of them.

I decided that it was time to get walking. I didn't want to stick around in one place for too long. Not only does it get boring, but people begin to wonder what your intentions are.

As I was leaving the Santa Cruz area I passed a sign that read Davenport 9 miles, Pescadero 34 miles, and San Francisco 76 miles. I was starting to wish that I hadn't taken those bus rides now. I could do 10 miles in two hours.

I definitely wasn't interested in staying in San Francisco. I only wanted to get there and get out. So, I would have to find somewhere that I could lay low for about two weeks. For now, though, I would just walk slow and check out the sights.

Just a few miles outside of Davenport, I noticed a beach access area. You had to climb up these steps that were made of logs to get up over the hill to the beach. There were only maybe six cars parked alongside the road, so I figured I would check it out.

When I got to the top of the hill, which was a set of train tracks that I assume were just for service trucks, I could tell that there were several people down below but I didn't pay them any mind. I was focused on staring out at the ocean. Then I hear what sounded like someone walking through the bushes next to me.

I turn to look and there's this lady with no clothes on. I didn't want to make this anymore awkward than it already was so I looked back down at the beach when I noticed everyone down there was naked. Oh, okay. This is a nude beach! Ha! Good thing I didn't don't go down there because I wasn't really in the mood to be taking my clothes off.

Actually, when I was in San Diego I was offered to come to a nude beach with this couple that had bought me lunch. The lady that made me the offer seemed kind of upset that I didn't want to go. It just wouldn't be fair to her if I went and got naked now.

While I'm thinking back to all of this naked nonsense, I was also offered the opportunity to partake in the adult the film industry. That was while I was in San Diego, too. They offered me $10,000 and I almost considered it because that was a lot of money.

I asked the people who were following my blog what they thought about it but when I mentioned the business's name it sent the company a flag. I had violated their terms of privacy and my deal was canceled. Probably for the best anyways.

I continued on into Davenport, passed Shark Fin Cove, and made my way down to another beach. I needed to rinse my face and shirt off because all of my sweat had turned into salt, and I was feeling a bit crusty.

The ocean was violent that day so I was lucky to find a cave where the ocean had pushed water into. The cave made a big loop that started at the edge of the ocean and made its way back closer to land. I went inside and laid down in the water for a few seconds. That's about all you could stand without a wet suit. It was mid-summer but the Pacific Ocean stays around 50 degrees.

I make my way back up to the road and head into town. It wasn't much of a town but I wasn't looking for anything other than a place to camp. I headed towards the ocean and made my way down onto this cliff.

There were plenty of trees and brush all around so I would be able to make a fire tonight. Where I was located, it was kind of like I was in a bowl and a bit difficult to make it down to. I wouldn't have to worry about being detected so I was able to relax.

I went ahead and put my tent up even though it was probably around 3:00 p.m. or so, and began collecting firewood. I did that for about two hours and pulled my sleeping pad out so I could just chill out and wait for it to get dark. It was quite cloudy that day. A bit dreary, actually. A nice day to be relaxing outside next to the ocean and I had this spot all to myself.

Around 6:00 p.m. I was lying there looking up at the clouds when I noticed a black spot. I thought it was a bird until I realized that it was just sitting there. I kept my eye on. It would disappear behind the clouds a few times but it never moved.

Within a few minutes there were three of them. I started to think back about what I had seen back in Carson City, Nevada and wondered if these were the same things, or even the same ones. I got a picture of one and then the three together, as well.

If these were UFOs then I wanted to keep what I was seeing as proof. My other pictures and videos that I had uploaded to my blog were gone and they were also gone from my phone. I uploaded these pictures to my blog and even sent them to several different email addresses.

They had been sitting overhead for about an hour now. Still in the same exact spot. I didn't know what to do or think about it. It was getting dark, though, so I went ahead to prepare my fire.

It felt like I had blinked and all of a sudden, I was inside of my tent. I sat up and realized that it was morning. I never even started my fire. The wood that I had stacked was all still there. I looked up to see if those black spots were still in the sky but they were gone.

I didn't know what else to think or do so I packed up and started my way for Pescadero. I took a picture next to a mile sign and realized that my earrings were gone. I had been wearing them for the past few years.

I had my ear lobes stretched and the ones that I had in my ears were screwed in on both sides so that they wouldn't fall out. It struck me as odd that they were all of a sudden gone after all of these years. I feel a little embarrassed to come out and say it but I'm pretty sure that I had been abducted by someone or something. Even if that were the case, why would they take my earrings?

It was 25 miles to Pescadero and I figured that would be a good walk for the day. I went to take a drink of water when I realized that it was all gone. This didn't make any sense either. I filled up before I left Santa Cruz and I never even touched my canteens. I only used those when my bladder was empty. All three of my water supplies were bone dry, though.

Once I made it into Pesacadero I realized that there wasn't anywhere to fill up on water so I decided to do 15 more miles into Half Moon Bay. I knew there would be places to fill up once I made it there so that was my motivation. This guy stops after I made it about 8 miles from Pescadero and asks if I needed a ride. He said he was going to San Francisco and didn't mind giving me a lift.

I had the guy drop me off in Half Moon Bay and then I

made my way over to a store to fill up on my water. Now, I can see if this place is going to suit me for about two weeks. I went down to the beach and followed it back south for about a mile or so. I found this spot that had been corroded out of the side of the cliff and decided that I would stay here until it was time for me to leave.

I stayed down there for about four days when Christy realized that I was nearby. She decided to come pick me up so I could crash at her place back in Woodland. When we got back to her place I almost immediately regretted my decision. I really liked Christy, her dog (Romeo), and all of her friends in Woodland; but it was about 120 degrees and I couldn't stand it.

I stayed with her for about four days before I finally gave in and got a bus back down to Half Moon Bay. If the weather would have been a bit more favorable, I would have loved staying; but that heat made it unbearable.

The bus that I took only made it to San Francisco. Then I had to take a subway down to the next bus station. I had never been in San Francisco or a subway so it was somewhat nerve-wracking. I took a step back and watched to see how everyone else got around on the subway. I got it all figured out pretty quick and I was back in Half Moon Bay before dark.

I didn't want to just sit at the beach for another week so I had to figure out something to keep myself occupied. I found a PVC pipe and decided to take it down to the beach and make a bow with it.

I made a fire and heated the PVC until it was nice and flexible. Then I shaped it into the look that I was going for. It's more about looks, though. Different shapes will give you different draw weights. I was looking for something around the 45lb range.

I remember later on that I had seen an old tent that had been ripped apart. I went back to it so I could check for any tent poles. I ended up finding a few but only one of them would be able to be used as an arrow. Then I went off into the forest just southeast of town.

Later on that night, I returned to my campsite to cook up a nice meal. Fresh meat was just what I needed to get my mind and body in the right state of mind. I'd bring my bow up to this lady's house in the morning. I talked to her a few days ago and she said her son's birthday was coming up. I figured I would give it to him as a gift.

The next morning, I made my way back into town to get some coffee and dropped the bow off on my way. The kid had a hard time drawing the bow back but the mom thought that it was a neat gift. When I got to the coffee shop the barista told me that I could get any drink I wanted. It was on the house! I should have gotten her name and number. She was really pretty and she knew the way to my heart. Nothing beats a nice-looking lady and a cup of coffee!

After I left the coffee shop I decided to walk around and noticed that there was a relay for life going on up at the school. I figured that would give me something to do for the next couple of days. I ended up walking for twenty-four hours and racking up about 100 miles.

While I was there I ran into a girl named Jen. The next day she asked if I wanted to hang out so I agreed to it. We went down to the beach and then she offered to bring me back to her place so I could do some laundry and get a shower.

After that, I went back down to my camping spot and just kind of hung out until it was time to go to sleep. I hadn't made a bow drill fire in a while and I wanted to make sure I still had it in me. A nice fire to keep me company was nice. While the fire was going I noticed that there was a golf ball in the sand. I decided to toss it in to see what would happen. It was pretty interesting, actually. Give it a try some time. Just make sure you have somewhere to run for safety.

The next day I went back into town for another coffee and ran into a man named Bill. He was a local homeless man but he was just an old hippie really. We talked a lot about health foods and things like that but I remember him saying how he had hung out with Charles Manson before he ended up in prison. He said that Manson had the craziest look in his eyes.

After I parted ways with Bill I went walking and ran into a lady named Elise. She let me come over to her house so I could get a shower and she made me lunch. I figured since she made me lunch I would make her a necklace. I thanked her and then I was on my way to meet up with Jen again.

When I met up with Jen we decided to get a motel room. She lived with her grandma and wanted to have a few beers. Basically, we were having a going away party because tomorrow I would be making my way to San Francisco so I could catch my flight up to Alaska.

There were a few days that I spent in Half Moon Bay that I decided to leave out. If something wasn't happening then, you know, I was just out walking around and camping. Nothing too exciting.

I do remember doing some dumpster diving a couple of times, though. I found about fifty bags of candy and about twenty DVDS. I didn't care much for the candy but I was amazed at how much there was. As for the DVDS? I ended up selling them.

Long story short, Half Moon Bay was a great place to kill some time. Everyone there seemed to be really nice and I even had my own man cave. Speaking of my man cave, I had turned it into quite the home. I had even built a table and chair down there. I don't know if it's all still there or not but if you find it, have fun! Until next time, I was heading for San Francisco.

I had made it half way to San Mateo, just west of the Upper Crystal Springs Reservoir, when I decided to stop where I was at. I didn't need to be in San Francisco until tomorrow afternoon and I had no interest in being in any cities.

I found a nice spot to camp and was even able to get a fire going. I could, theoretically, have a fire any time that I wanted, but I had to make sure that it would go undetected. I knew how to build a Dakota Fire but it wasn't like I was trying THAT hard to not be found.

It was still pretty early so I began walking around. I wasn't looking for anything in particular but I came across a rattlesnake. I figured since I was planning on having a fire tonight that I'd go ahead and have this guy for dinner. It's always weird to me, eating snakes. They have kind of an earthy/fishy taste that I like but the cleaning part has always kind of irked me. The way their muscles tense up seems to give their body life, even though you know they're dead.

That morning I made my way back out to the main road and headed over to San Mateo. I noticed that I could take a train from here up to the airport so I decided to go ahead and hop on it. I had a few hours to catch my plane but I didn't want something to happen between now and then. My plane was leaving at 11:30 a.m. and I needed to have some time to get through security, too.

It was July 29, 2015 and I had boarded my plane for Anchorage, Alaska. I couldn't believe it. I wanted to visit Alaska for as long as I could remember. I hadn't just planned on visiting, though. I wanted to find a place to start a new life for myself.

Walking is a lot different than flying. If I had been walking it would have all slowly built itself around me. When you're flying, though, you jump from one extreme to another in just a matter of hours. I wondered if I was mentally prepared to be dropped off in Alaska with nothing but my backpack.

I finally arrived in Anchorage, AK around 5:00 p.m. and walked away from the airport. The air felt thinner and cleaner compared to anywhere else I had been. When I say "thinner" I mean that in a way that it didn't feel polluted and humid. Though, the humidity is quite high in Alaska, it didn't have the mugginess because of the low dew points.

As I was walking into Anchorage, I got a message from a girl named Katy. She said that she wanted to hang out and could meet me at one of the stores nearby. I just needed to wait there for about thirty minutes and she would swing by to pick me up in her friend's truck.

When she got there, we greeted one another with a hug and then we made our way down towards Chugach State Park. We continued on a little farther than that, though. We found a turnout about fifteen miles from the park.

After we stopped the truck, Katie handed me a six pack of beer. It was one of my favorite beers, too! She had been following me on my blog for a while so she knew what I liked. That was really thoughtful of her.

Then we walked up onto this large hill and looked out into the Gulf of Alaska. Well, if you want to get technical, this part of the gulf is known as the Turnagain Arm. The Gulf of Alaska just wraps its way around the Kenai Peninsula. Either way, I was in Alaska and this spot was beautiful!

It was about 9:00 p.m. when we left. Katie dropped me off in Anchorage and she went back to her apartment. She was living with a friend, otherwise she probably would have invited me over.

I had absolutely no idea where I was going to spend the night. I walked around for a while and ended up crashing next to someone's house. I tried to keep hidden by placing my tent between their backyard fence and a few bushes.

When I was packing up the next morning, I noticed a man was walking around in his yard. He looked over at me and said "I wondered who the hell was camping in my yard. You didn't seem to be bothering anything, though, so I didn't wake you." I apologized and told him that I had just made it into Anchorage and didn't have any time to figure the area out yet. He didn't mind and even asked if I needed anything. I told him that I was fine but thanked him for letting me sleep in his yard.

I needed to find a place where I could camp without intruding on people's property. So, I started looking in all of the wooded areas around Anchorage. It became apparent very quickly that Anchorage had a huge homeless population. I didn't mind their business but I knew this was going to cause me problems.

When cities have a large homeless community and the majority of them are on drugs, alcoholics, responsible for violent crimes, and all that is bad; then people are going to associate me with them. It's sad but that's just the way it is. I had a backpack and I was guilty.

I swing by this gas station to get some coffee and a breakfast burrito. After I left, I walked around to the side to sit and enjoy my breakfast. The manager comes outside and tells me to leave and that if he ever sees me around here again he would call the police. I couldn't even explain myself to him.

Alright, I need to get my identification changed so that I'm a resident. Then I can leave Anchorage and not have to worry about this mess. I had to have an address before I could get a new identification, though. Now, where was I going to get an address? I had some thinking to do.

I made my way over to a park on the northwest side of Anchorage. A hiking trail started here. I followed this trail for about two miles and found a place that I could camp and keep hidden from everyone.

Camping was a little hard when I first got into Anchorage. It got dark around midnight but then the sun was coming up just three hours later. I had been using the sun as sleep schedule but that wasn't the case here. I was waking up constantly so I could check and see what time it was.

I knew there was a homeless shelter not too far from where I was. It was called Beans Cafe. I wondered if I would be able to use their address to get my new identification so I made my over.

When I to the homeless shelter there was a dead guy

lying on the sidewalk. People were all walking around him like it was no big deal. I stood there for a minute and heard someone say that the ambulance was on their way. There wasn't anything I could do so I made my way inside. When I walked in they yelled at me, "WE DON'T DO SHOWERS TODAY AND WE DON'T HAVE ANY ROOMS AVAILABLE!"

I replied, "Oh, well, thanks for the information but I was just wondering if there was a way that I could get an address from you guys? I need to change my address since I just moved here and need somewhere to get my mail and have my identification changed".

The man rolled his eyes and screamed for one of the other workers to come and answer my question. The lady that came over wrote down their address on a piece of paper and handed it to me. I thanked her and made my way to the post office to have my address changed.

The address change went well but I had to wait a few days for the proof letter to come in before I could get my new ID. I decided to go check some other areas away from the city while I waited. I was heading out of town when I met up with Katie again. She had the day off and had her friend drop her off so we could go adventuring together.

Before we went off to explore we decided to grab us a bite to eat at a pizza restaurant. There was a long wait but it was worth it. The pizza was great. The beer was great. We got along great. Now, that we've had some food and beers in our bellies it was time to go have some fun. It's always more fun when you have friends!

We walked a few miles towards the east side of town. It had been all wooded area for a while and we came across a creek that went off into the forest. We followed the creek for a while and decided to make a small fire. I can't remember why we were making a fire, though. Probably just because we could.

We found a nice place to sit and chat and building a fire would give us something to do instead of just sitting there.

It would help to get rid of the mosquitoes, too! That was probably the main reason we wanted to build a fire now that I look back at it.

I was cutting some dead branches down when I almost whacked my finger off. I wasn't swinging my machete all that hard (luckily) since the branches were dead, but I kept all of my blades razor sharp.

I looked down and my left hand middle finger, surprised to see that it was still there, and noticed that I had filleted the flesh down to the bone. The only thing that kept me from completely removing all of the skin was my finger nail.

It was bleeding pretty bad so I rinsed it off, put the skin back over the bone, and wrapped one of my bandannas around it. I most certainly needed stitches but I didn't feel like going to the hospital. It would be fine as long as it didn't get infected.

I walked Katie back home after that and then I was on my own again. I didn't want to go back into the city but I had some business to take care of. I knew it would be a few days to get my address change letter and then another few days to get my ID. Hopefully, the city wouldn't drive me crazy before then. I went back to my spot on the trail and called it a day.

The next few days I spent my time walking around and each passing day I became more and more agitated. Everywhere I went I was either being chased off by homeless people or businesses. I was losing a lot of sleep because most nights I would hear people fighting, gun shots going off, and police sirens or ambulances. I have bipolar and PTSD so this was the absolute worst place for me.

I get a message from Katie and she asks if I'd like to go with her and her friend up to Fairbanks. She didn't have to ask me twice. Get me out of Anchorage!

On our way up to Fairbanks, we made a few stops to get out and go hiking. Katie was all into hiking like I was but her friend was more of a city girl and chose to stay in the truck while we went exploring.

We pulled over at this one area that had a hiking trail. We didn't want to go off too far but just wanted to get out and stretch our legs. Katie's friend took a nap while we went for a walk.

We noticed that there were blueberries everywhere and we kept walking and picking them. Eventually, we ran into a lady who had been out picking berries all day and had a few buckets full. She had a dog with her and the dog kept trying to follow us, but after we made it so far, the dog ran back to its owner.

We had probably walked about a mile when the fields turned into thick brush. You seriously wouldn't be able to see a bear if it was three feet away from you. That's how dense the brush up there is.

I noticed something brown sticking out onto the trail up ahead. I thought it might be a bear so I put my arm out and made Katie stop. Then a large moose steps out with its baby. I said "Katie. Don't move. If this thing charges us, run behind the trees."

The moose and her baby were probably thirty feet away from us when this happened. They turn to look at us and they're just standing there, looking at us. We stood there for about thirty seconds before the mother and baby continued on into the bush on the other side of the trail. Katie wanted to go follow them but I told her that we just got lucky. Unless you want to get kicked to death you'd best just leave a moose alone.

We walk back to the car and continue on up to Fairbanks. Katie and her friend didn't realize that I had taken several of my anxiety medications before they offered to bring me with them. I was really starting to feel it now. I was pretty good at hiding the fact that I was messed up but my judgment was definitely off. Way off.

We stopped at a store along the way and I bought a case of beer. I ended up drinking most of them on our way into Fairbanks. They still had no idea how messed up I really was. Then they decided to stop and see one of their friends at a bar. I had a few more drinks while I was there and took a few more of my pills. They had no idea about me taking my pills, though.

When we left the bar, I finished off the rest of the beer that I had and passed out. I woke up the next morning and had no idea where we were. Katie and her friend were still asleep. I realized that I had pissed myself so I got out and tried to get everything cleaned up.

I noticed that we were parked at a church so I decided to go in so I could change my clothes. When I went into the bathroom I noticed there was a shower so I took advantage of that. I got myself cleaned up and took care of my laundry, too.

When I came out of the bathroom there were people all standing around. They were asking what I had been in there doing because the bride was trying to get ready for her wedding. I didn't know what to do besides apologize. I didn't know someone was getting married!

I walk back out to the truck and Katie and her friend are looking at me like they were looking at a ghost. "Dude! You died last night! When we woke up you were gone! What happened? Where have you been?" I couldn't believe that I had died but I told them we need to leave because these people are mad. I just made a bride late for her wedding.

Apparently, I was passed out for a while and when they hit a bump my head smacked against the window and dash. My body was completely limp. Katie held onto me so I wouldn't keep hitting everything. They came here to get some sleep and have a few drinks themselves. When they got back into the truck to sleep they realized that I had no pulse.

They had been drinking and didn't want to drive. There was no cell service where we were at. It seemed like it was too late to do anything about it except to wait until the morning to drive me to the hospital.

I doubt that I was dead but I'm sure my heart rate had plummeted drastically. I was super healthy, so my normal resting heart rate was around forty-eight beats per minute. I decided to not mix my medication with alcohol ever again, though. I knew I shouldn't have been but, like I said, I wasn't thinking straight.

Somehow, though, I didn't even have a hangover. As a matter of fact, I felt great and was ready to do whatever they wanted. They said they had been invited over to one of their friend's house and they were grilling out and stuff. So, we made our way to their house.

There weren't a whole lot of people there but they all seemed really nice. We just hung and talked until it started to get close to dark and then we all began gathering wood for the fire. They already had several logs cut and dried for the winter so we used a few of those. I was put in charge of building the fire. They were amazed at how fast I got it up and going. I swore by it that I could start a fire faster than someone with a lighter. I still stand by that to this day!

As we were all sitting around the fire, this little girl comes up and asks me if I know how to ride a unicycle. I told her I didn't but wondered why she asked. She said, "We have one over there but no one knows how to ride it." I asked her to bring it over and I'd see what I could do.

The first time I tried to ride this one-wheeled beast I landed flat on my back. Everyone was laughing but I expected to fall the first few times at least. The second time, I almost fell but I caught myself because I had gotten the feel for it. The third time, I got a few pedals in before I got bucked off. By my fourth try, I pretty much had it down. I wasn't ready for a circus but I had learned how to ride a unicycle! Everyone was impressed because a lot of people had tried it and no one else had ever been able to get it. The little girl was ecstatic about my newly acquired skills.

I had always been curious about bow hunting bears and asked if anyone here had any experience with that. One of the guys there said he had tried it a few times but always ended up needing to pull his rifle out to finish the job. I told him that I had already started working on a bow back near Anchorage and I planned on taking it with me when I went up into Denali National Park.

He looked at me kind of funny and said, "making it?" I had found a great piece of Yew that was perfect for making a longbow. I had spent a few hours here and there carving and shaping it on a jig that I had made. I didn't plan on hunting any bears with it but I didn't have a rifle and wanted something other than my bear spray. I did need a weapon for hunting, though. It was either going to be a long bow or an atlatl. I hadn't decided on which I wanted to bring with me yet.

It was getting late and so I decided to turn in for the night. I went and got my tent set up off to the side of their backyard. Katie asked if I would mind if she slept in the tent with me. I would be crazy to deny a fine lady from sleeping in my tent. It felt nice to have someone to cuddle with. That did wonders from all of the stress that I had been going through.

The next morning, we made our way back down for Anchorage. I wasn't looking forward to it but I still had some preparations to do before making my way out into the bush. On our way back down, I had them stop near Denali so I could get out and get a good feel for what was in store for me. The vastness was almost overwhelming but I'd rather be out there than in the city.

When we got back to Anchorage, Katie and her friend let me come with them to their apartment so I could get a shower and then I was back on my own again. I went back to where I had been working on my bow and realized that it was gone. That was kind of a bummer. I wasn't all that surprised, though. Homeless people were walking around 24/7 and if they see anything they will take it.

When I left Katie's apartment I noticed that side of Anchorage didn't seem so bad. I headed back across the bridge and camped close to the Elmendorf Air Force Base. I didn't have any issues over here except for this one time someone thought I was using their power outlet to charge my phone, but no, I was using my solar panel!

I stayed in that area for a couple of nights but during the day I was going into town so I could eat lunch at the homeless shelter. I stuck out like a sore thumb in that place. Not to be judgmental but I was the only one that didn't appear to be on drugs.

I admit that I had begun abusing my medications and started drinking heavily but that was short lived. If you were in my shoes you probably would have done the same thing.

Most of these people were on some really hard drugs, though, and stayed drunk all day every day. Just about every time I went down there I saw someone who had died during the night. It certainly was a depressing place to go for lunch every day but I couldn't complain about the food. I needed to hurry up and get out of there.

I found a wooded area outside of Anchorage and began working on a small cabin. I spent about a month on it, coming and going into town only as needed. It was going great until some group of homeless punks followed me out there. I never saw them actually following me but they must have. There was no reason for anyone to be where I was. That's why I was there.

I didn't plan on staying out here permanently but I wanted something to get me through the winter if I hadn't found a place before then. The only thing that I hadn't finished yet was the roof, so I was pretty upset that I had been followed. It wasn't just that I had been discovered but I was attacked.

I went into town one day to pick up some nails. My tent and all of my gear was back at the cabin I had been working on. When I returned I noticed that there was a girl in my tent. I asked her what she was doing and she said "Oh, I'm just trying to find my phone".

I replied, "Why would your phone be in my tent?" I pulled my bear spray out and aimed it at her face. I looked in my tent and realized that pretty much everything was gone. I asked her where all of my stuff was at and she said she didn't know. I yelled at her "BULLSHIT! YOU AREN'T OUT HERE BY YOURSELF! DO YOU THINK I'M FUCKING STUPID? WHERE ARE YOUR PUNK ASS FRIEND'S AND WHERE DID THEY TAKE MY STUFF?"

Then I hear some rustling in the woods and thought that it was a bear that I had seen several times out here, but it was two men. When they saw me, they began running towards me with my bowie knife and my machete. I wasn't scared. I was pissed off. I stood there and waited for my moment.

When they got close I turned and hosed them down with my bear spray. I was so mad that the bear spray didn't even bother me but they were rolling around and screaming. The girl was back behind me on her knees coughing and trying to rub the bear spray off of her face. I tossed my bowie knife and machete over to the side and pulled some zip ties out of my pocket to cuff the two men. Then I checked to see if they had any of my things on them.

I gathered up my tent, knife, and machete and told the girl to take me to my stuff. She said "Okay! Just please don't hit me!". I told her that I wasn't going to hit her but if she didn't take me to my things then I was about to hose her down like I did her friends.

We walked through the woods for about a hundred yards and found all of my things scattered about. I had been living out of this pack for a while. I knew every single item that was in my pack. I looked around to see if anything was missing. It was all there. I told the woman to go help her friends before they go blind. I gathered my things and never went back.

I was so mad that I was shaking. I was so sick of Anchorage. I wasn't even in Anchorage but they had followed me out here. I was miles outside of Anchorage and I still had to deal with this crap. I shook it off and gathered my composure. I noticed that my band aid had fallen off during that scuffle and my finger looked like it might be infected so I decided to walk to the emergency room.

After they told me that my finger wasn't infected, and that I had done a good job at keeping it clean and sealed properly, I told them about the incident that had just happened. They told me not to worry about it. They said it was in self-defense and they deserved it. If someone came in from bear spray burns then they would know where they got it from and they would notify the police if I wanted to press charges. I told them that wasn't necessary.

8

After I left the hospital I made my way into town. I wanted to grab a bite to eat so I decided to stop by one of the restaurants that I had passed by a few times. It seemed like a nice place to have dinner and relax. I could really use it after what had happened today.

I made my way to the back-door entrance and there was a security guard standing there. He told me that I couldn't bring my backpack inside so I left it sitting out. I figured it would be safe since he had asked me not to bring it in and he was guarding the area.

I went in and took a seat. The waitress comes over and takes my order. While I'm waiting for my food to come out the security guard comes in and tells me that I have to leave. I asked him why and he said it was because I was going to eat and run. I told him that I wasn't and showed him my ID and credit card.

He asked if that was my backpack outside. I said, "Yes. It is." He said, "I'm sorry but I know how you people are. Don't get mad because I caught you. Get your shit and go." Wow! I told him that I had ordered my food and after I finish my dinner I will leave.

Another security guard comes up and they both grab

me. They pull me out through the back door and throw me onto the concrete, causing me to get a gash on the back of my head. Then they threw my backpack and trekking poles at me and told me to get out of there before they called the cops.

I had purchased a camera for $300 before I got here and opened my pack to see if it was damaged. It wasn't just damaged but it was completely destroyed. I barely had any money to begin with and spent a large portion of it on this camera so I could share good quality photos with people.

I was on the verge of going back inside to fight the security guards but I didn't want to go to jail. I was so close to a breaking point and everyone just kept pushing my buttons. I couldn't take it anymore. I walked back across the bridge to my old camping spot. Tomorrow I'll be making my way for Denali.

I began walking the next morning and made it to Wasilla when a lady pulls up and asks if I needed a ride. I asked her where she was heading and she told me she was going up to Fairbanks. I said, "Perfect! You can drop me off at Byers Lake if you don't mind?"

I got in and as we were driving she said, "Byers Lake, huh? They have a nice campground. How long you plan on staying? I have to come back through in a few days if you need a ride back down to Wasilla." I replied, "They have a campground? I might stay there tonight but I'm going into Denali." She asked, "By yourself? Do you have a gun? The bears are pretty bad out that way."

I told her that I didn't have a gun but I wasn't worried about any bears. I was more worried about the people back in Anchorage. She laughed but she had no idea what I'd been through.

When she dropped me off near the campground I noticed there were a few people hanging around. I didn't feel like being around anyone. I needed to be completely isolated for a while. I walked until I found a spot where I could cross the Susitna River. It didn't take me that long, actually.

As soon as I crossed the bridge I felt like I was in a completely different world. No one knew where I was except for the lady that just dropped me off. It was a great feeling but an eerie feeling at the same time.

Either way, I would rather be out here than be in Anchorage. I kept walking, navigating through thick brush and a few creeks. It wasn't long before I came up to Spink Lake. I didn't know what lake it was at the time but I've since found it on a map.

There were two Grizzly Bears fighting next to the beach. They were probably fifty yards from me when I finally saw them but I had been hearing their roars for a while. I couldn't tell what they were fighting over but I assumed that it was food. I watched them for about five minutes and decided that I'd best be on my way because they might not be fighting for too much longer.

There were some mountains to the northwest so I headed in that direction. I made it into the hills just as it was getting dark and sat up camp. I didn't know if I wanted to start a fire or not because the smoke might attract those bears that I had seen but I went ahead and made one anyways.

The next morning, I made my way higher up to get a better view of everything. From up here I got a better idea of what I was up against if I wanted to make it to Denali. A lot of the mountains looked really steep and jagged. Denali didn't look far away but I knew that it would take me at least a week to get there.

I continued hiking for a few days, trying to make my way up to Denali, when I was charged by a grizzly bear for the first time. I tried to stay away from the creeks unless I needed water because I had seen several of them, and they were always walking along the creeks.

The bear charged at me but it stopped before making contact. It happened so fast but somehow, I already had my bear spray and bowie knife drawn. It kept smacking the ground and huffing. I started kicking at the ground and screaming. I don't think I've ever screamed so loud in my life. I was hesitant to use my bear spray because I didn't want to make matters worse. Started to slowly walk backwards and it started walking towards me. That's when I sprayed him down.

The bear started acting crazy and I thought it was going to attack me. This was a new can that I had picked up before I came out here and I had used the whole thing on this one bear. It finally ran off but now I don't have any more bear spray. I began walking back up into the hills that I had come down from and felt like maybe I should go back into Anchorage. I definitely needed to get a rifle.

It took me three days to make it back to the road. Thankfully, I hadn't run into anymore bears since that one. I don't know what would have happened if I didn't have that bear spray but I have a pretty good guess!

When I made it onto the highway I found my way back to the campground. I was hoping to catch a ride into Anchorage but there weren't any people here this time so I started walking. It wasn't long before a truck came up behind me. It was a man and he was drunk. I normally wouldn't get into a vehicle with someone who had been drinking but beggars can't be choosers.

He wasn't going into Anchorage but I had made it back down to Wasilla. I started walking back to Anchorage but decided to go check out Eklutna Lake first. It was only about six miles from the highway and I really wasn't ready to go into the city yet.

It was beautiful out here! I should had just come here to begin with! I was walking around and considered staying out here for a few days. That's when I saw another grizzly. This one hadn't noticed me and I wanted it to stay that way. When I saw him, he was grabbing and clawing at a tree. I was probably seventy-five yards away but I could still hear the tree being ripped apart.

I turned to walk back to the road. I kept looking back to make sure he wasn't following me. He probably would have run off if he did see me but I had just been charged a few days ago and I wasn't in the mood to go through with that again.

Once I made it back into Anchorage I went to a bar and grill called McGinley's Pub (very friendly) for dinner when I ran into a few other army infantry vets. They let me have dinner with them and it felt nice to be with a group of people who I could relate with. We shared a lot of military stories and had some good laughs.

After they left I got on Craigslist to look for any rifles for sale. Just out of curiosity I clicked on housing and noticed there was a dry cabin up in Willow for just $500 a month. I had a crowd funding site set up where people who were following me could help out if they wanted over the years. I ended up raising $5,000 over the course of the trip but most of that had gone into gear, paying my phone bill, food, a motel room here and there, or just whatever I needed to keep going. I had a lot of support from my followers, obviously.

I started that at the beginning of my journey so it wasn't like I had that much in there all at once. I did have about $700 left in there that I was trying to save for emergencies. I figured that I would give the owners of this cabin a call and let them know that I was interested. Then I could probably find a job and make this cabin work but they said that someone had already claimed it.

Winter was on the way and I didn't know how I felt about going back out into Denali, even if I did get a rifle. I didn't have the time to build another cabin and even if I did it would be considered squatting, which was basically what I was doing the first time I built a cabin. You can't just wander off and build a cabin unless you own the land.

I felt like my timing and luck had reached its limit. I

ordered a plane ticket back to Tennessee but I picked a flight thirty days in advance. This way I still had time to see if I could make things work, but if I couldn't then I knew I had something to fall back on. It just seemed like the best thing to do.

I found a place to camp in the woods within Anchorage and then the next day I ran into a lady named Ashley. We hung out pretty much all day and then she asked if I wanted to come back to her place. I agreed to it. Anything to get me off of these streets! That, and she was a nice person.

She lived with her son, brother, and mom. We all got along really well. We all had the same sense of humor and they were really down to earth people. They were upset by how I had been treated in Anchorage but they knew how bad the streets here were. My backpack just made me look like one of the bad guys.

I stayed with Ashley and her family for a few days and then she and her brother asked if I'd like to go with them to a concert. I can't remember where we went but it took us about six hours to get there. I wasn't really paying attention to where we were going because I was in the back, playing harmonica for their dog. He would howl while I was playing. They got a video of it but I'm not sure whatever happened to it.

When we get to where ever it was, we went up to this pavilion in a park where the bands were playing. There was a school and a gas station so it was a pretty small town. I think there were about forty people there at the pavilion.

The bands were playing metal music, which I did not expect. I grew up playing in metal bands so it was entertaining to me but everyone else seemed to be uninterested. I thought their lack of enthusiasm was funny so I got a picture of them. Just imagine two people standing there like zombies in front of a band playing some heavy metal music. Well, I thought it was funny.

After that they let me drive back home because

Ashley's brother wanted to take a nap. I hadn't driven in a while and I didn't even know where we were. It's pretty hard to get lost in Alaska, though. If you stick to the highways you'll eventually end up in Anchorage. It was pretty much a straight shot. As long as you don't hit a moose or a drunk driver then it's smooth sailing.

We finally get back to Ashley's house and I crash on the couch. I don't know why but a wave of depression hit me like a ton of bricks. I ended up sleeping on their couch for about three days. They didn't seem to mind but I felt like I was being bad company so I thanked them for letting me hang around and I took off.

I headed back into town and made my way for Katie's neighborhood again. I found this building across from a gas station and put my tent up in the back. I stayed in my tent for about two weeks. I only walked over to the gas station maybe two times during those two weeks to fill up on water. Besides that, I was just lying there.

I finally motivated myself to get up and go do something. I had about a week left before my plane was supposed to leave. If I could find some reason to stay then I would. I owed it to myself to give Alaska a chance. I had made it here and didn't want to give up so easily.

As I'm crossing the bridge back into Anchorage I notice that there is no traffic. Not that there was ever a lot of traffic coming across the bridge but there was absolutely none. I also noticed there were several helicopters flying around the city. I didn't know what to think. I just wanted to get to the homeless shelter so I could eat some lunch.

I was skeptical but I continued across the bridge anyways. I was about halfway when a police officer pulls up and tells me to get in the car. I asked him why and he said, "Get in the car now. The president is about to cross this bridge and this is a high-risk area."

So, I get into the police car and he drives me to the end of the bridge where I was. He told me not to move until the president had passed. I stood there for about ten minutes and I noticed several vehicles are coming towards me across the bridge. This must be the president.

Talk about feeling awkward. I just got escorted off of the bridge because I made it unsafe for the president to cross and now I'm standing on the side of the road. There's no one on this side of Anchorage. There aren't any cars or people around. It's just me. Standing there by myself with a backpack.

After the president passes I begin walking into town and head for the homeless shelter. I hadn't eaten in a few days and I was expecting to go for a pretty long hike. Rice, carrots, two tortilla shells, a side of more rice, a piece of lettuce, and a cookie. This should be enough to get me to where I want to go.

I had my sights set on Flattop Mountain. It wasn't too far out of the way but it would give me an idea of what that area was like. If I felt like I could wander off then I would. I made it just a few miles from the trail head before dark and found a church that I decided to camp behind.

It was weird because I had been here for almost four months. When I got here it got dark at midnight and the sun came up just a few hours later. Now it's getting dark at 8:00 p.m. and the sun is coming up at 8:00 a.m.

The seasons changed so fast up here. It happened before I even noticed that it was changing. It was like one day everything was green and the next day everything had turned colors. I've never experienced such a rapid change in season as I had in Alaska. I knew that winter was about to come sooner than I thought.

The next morning, I wandered off of from the road because I just wanted to be in the woods. It made me feel better. I was still heading up to Flattop Mountain but I wanted to make my own way instead of following some trail. I wasn't too far away and all I had to do was head east.

It was mostly uphill at this point so I decided to take a break and eat a granola bar. I picked a box up just before I left town because I didn't know how long I was going to be out here, what my chances were of trapping if it came to that, or whatever else. It's always nice to have some backup food. As I was sitting there I heard something walking around in the woods. I was pretty certain that it was a bear. It probably smelled my granola bar so I threw it on the ground and made my way up to higher ground.

I got behind a tree and waited to see what was making its way through the brush. I made it out of there just in time because out pops a large black bear. He didn't notice me, though. I was up on this hill and he had his head down. I could tell that he was trying to sniff out that granola bar.

I had broken the granola bar up into a lot of small pieces and spit out whatever was in my mouth. He eventually found it and began pecking at all of the little pieces. I watched him for about two minutes and got a couple of pictures of him. I knew he'd be hanging around for a while. I could tell he didn't care about anything else. I felt like I was safe as long as I didn't make too much noise. I backed out of there and left him to his trail magic.

I went back to the road because walking through the woods seemed a bit risky. I wanted to put some distance between me and that bear without making too much noise. I made it to the road and continued on my way up to the mountain.

When I got there, I reached a parking lot full of cars and people. I wasn't surprised, though. This was probably one of the easiest mountains to gain access to just outside of the city limits. I made my way to the top of the mountain and overlooked the city to my west, the gulf to my south, and the mountains to my east. I didn't know what to do next. I didn't want to go back into Anchorage, though, so I wandered off into the hills.

I spent a few days in the hills just east of Flattop Mountain and I loved it but I knew that winter was coming and I wasn't prepared for it. There was no way to prepare for it. I got here too late and the cabin that I had started on, while it could have been finished, was probably taken over. I accepted the hand that was dealt to me and made my way for the airport.

I took my time getting into Anchorage, though. I didn't want to be there any earlier than I had to be. I had one day until my flight left when I decided to camp not too far from the airport. While I was looking for a place to camp I was approached by a man who asked me if I knew where he could get any meth and he kept following me around. He eventually went away, though.

I went off and camped in the woods along the hiking trail that I had camped near a few times. This time I was just farther down the trail. It was raining really hard that night and around 2:00 a.m. I hear some man screaming. He kept yelling, "HEY! HEY, YOU WANNA FUCK WITH ME? YOU WANNA FUCK WITH ME? I'LL FUCKING KILL YOU!" He just kept repeating that over and over. He was standing on the trail a few feet away from my tent and I started to wonder if he was yelling at me because I never heard anyone else.

I poked my head out of my tent and the man was just standing there yelling all of this at himself. There was no one else around and he never saw me. He began to walk away but continued screaming. I was relieved to know that this was my last night in Anchorage, AK.

It was the morning of September 3, 2015 and I packed up and headed for the airport. I made it just in time to catch my plane which made leaving Alaska easier on me. It felt kind of like jumping into a lake. You know it's cold but once you're in it, it isn't so bad. I wanted Alaska to work out for me but I just wasn't prepared for it. I may return one day and give it another try. I felt like I was just in the wrong place at the wrong time. This was okay, though. I had a backup plan and I was already making phone calls.

After I landed in Nashville, Tennessee I hitch hiked back to my parent's house in Greenfield. I told them that I wouldn't be here long. I was just scooping up my friend, Mike. "What happened with Alaska?", my mom asked. I told her it was a long story and that she could read about it later.

Mike had put in his two-week notice at the job he was working at and then he was going to walk across America with me for St Jude Children's Research Hospital. He went ahead and bought his bus ticket for Florida and I found a week's worth of work laying down a foundation. Then I ordered my bus ticket, too.

We had three days to make it down to Jackson, Tennessee to catch our bus once we started walking. His sister dropped him off with me in Greenfield the day before so we could get an early start. It was only forty-five miles to the bus station. I figured this would be a good test walk for Mike.

Everything goes well on our way down to the bus station and we're on our way to Florida. It sounds like it all happened so fast because it really did. When I told him that I was leaving Alaska and wanted to walk across America, he was all in and ready to go.

We got to my uncle's house in Ft Walton Beach, Florida sometime in late September. I wanted to start our walk on October 1st but it was just way too hot. We ended up staying until November 1st, which wasn't a bad thing. Mike had never been to the beach so we spent most of our days just hanging out at the ocean.

We made it about twenty miles our first day and Mike finally got his first blister. I understand the pain that these blisters cause but they are means for celebrating. The more blisters you get and the faster you get them then the better off you will be. It's just hard to see it that way when your foot is on fire.

We crossed the bridge into Navarre and slept right on the sand in front of the ocean. When we woke up every was covered in sand and our things were soaking wet. Our main goal was to sleep undetected, though, not comfortably.

The next morning, we made our way for Pensacola Beach. Mike had a really hard time walking on his new blister so it took us nearly all day. He even felt like giving up a few times but I promised him that it would get better.

We kept our focus on this hotel that was about fifteen miles away. It felt like it never got any closer but we finally made it! We had a hard time finding a place to sleep once we got there, though. Because we wanted to use our tents we had to find a spot that was either hidden or far enough away from everyone. We ended up walking down the beach for almost a mile before we felt satisfied.

The next day we were headed for Pensacola. We stopped in Gulf Breeze for about an hour because the bridge coming up was intimidating. There was a lot of traffic and not a lot of shoulder. Mike was really nervous and just watched my feet until I told him to look over into the water.

There was a school of sting rays and they were all getting ganged up on by some sharks. Neither of us had ever seen anything like that. We had to cock her heads to look, though. If we turned our bodies a vehicle would have hit our backpacks. That's how close the traffic was. I even felt a truck graze my shirt once!

After we made it across the bridge it we hung out at the Veterans Memorial Park. We planned on sleeping there but decided to sit until it got dark before pulling our gear out. While we were sitting there this man comes up and offers to take us out to eat.

The man takes us to eat at one of his favorite barbecue restaurants and then brings us back down to the park. He knew we were planning on sleeping there but he gave us both some really weird vibes so we decided to keep walking until we found a more secluded area. We ended up doing some night walking and made it down to the Big Lagoon State Park.

It was dark when we got down there but we decided to

go back as far as we could without getting into the trees or being too noticeable. People were coming and going with their vehicles but no one ever came over to where we were at.

When we woke up we noticed there was a sign that read, "BEWARE OF ALLIGATORS". That was pretty funny because we were camping right next to the sign and even made jokes about alligators before we fell asleep.

The next day we made it to Gulf Shores, Alabama and still had plenty of daylight left. My friend Sydney was back living just a few miles north of here in Foley but this would be our last day next to the beach so we decided to go ahead and crash here. Tomorrow we would get to hang out with Sydney and be able to crash at her place.

We got up to Foley and troubles finding Sydney's address. It turned out that we were at the gas station right in front of her apartments. She was about to run across the street to come see me but I told her to stay where she was because I didn't want to see her get hit by another car.

Me and Mike take turns getting showers and then Sydney and her boyfriend take us to this bar across the street and we grab a few drinks. While we were having our drinks, I talked about how we slept next to that alligator warning sign and she said they knew where some alligators were around here.

I told them if we found one then I was going to wrestle it. I told them I was serious but I don't know if I actually would have. I probably would, though, knowing me. We went out later that night to see if we could find one but we never did. It was probably better that way.

We went back to their apartment and went crab fishing. It was surprisingly easy to catch crab where they were living. It didn't take long and we each had four of them to bring back into the house to have for dinner. They sure went down well with friends and a cold beer.

The next day me and Mike made our way to Barnwell instead of taking the shorter route up to Spanish Fort. We had kind of a slow day and ended up sleeping behind a store before we made it to Barnwell. We thought we had it made until around midnight I feel something sniffing at my head. I thought it was a bear and I smacked at it and yelled for it to get out of there.

Then we hear someone whistle for their dog. I open up my tent and there are two police officers. They start freaking out because they didn't expect anyone to be back here and it was illegal for them to let their dog just run like that. They were surprised that their dog didn't attack me. If it did they would have had a huge lawsuit on their hands.

They agreed to not say anything about us camping here if we agreed to not say anything about them letting their dog run loose. We figured that was a fair trade because they could still get us for trespassing since we didn't get permission from the store owner. I know exactly where we were at but I'm not going to say because we could have been anywhere and I don't want that to come back and cause any troubles for anyone.

We got up and out of there before the store opened and made our way for Barnwell. It started raining so we put our rain gear on. It was an unusually hot fall that year and Mike kept telling me that he thought his rain gear was leaking. When it stopped raining he took his jacket off and nearly a gallon of sweat came pouring out!

I told him not to wear his rain gear anymore because he was going to end up having a heat stroke. As hot as it was it would have felt great to walk through the rain anyways. No one likes being wet but I'm pretty sure he would have been better off just going without. All part of the experience, Mike!

We finally get into Barnwell and fill up on water. I got a cup of coffee and made Mike drink two liters of water before we could leave. Then we began heading north up towards Spanish Fort and crossed over into Mobile.

We didn't stop in Mobile, though. It just wasn't the right place for us. We kept walking, claimed our

Mississippi sign, and went until it was close to dark. As we grew tired and sore we figured we would camp off in the woods in the De Soto National Forest.

We pulled out a few little packs of food for dinner. I ate a lot less than Mike so I was done before him. After I finished eating I went and buried my garbage about fifty yards away. I told him to do the same thing because there are black bears in this area.

I fell asleep and then I woke to the sound of something making its way through the woods. I got up immediately and saw a black bear standing about twenty feet behind my tent. I began screaming and throwing sticks at it and it started to back off a little bit not much. Mike then wakes up and asks me why I'm screaming.

I yelled, "Mike! There's a bear out here! Get up! Now!" He replied, "Man, it's probably just a car or something." I yell again, "No! Mike! There is a bear right over there! I'm looking right at it!" I finally get sick of this bear not running away so I begin running towards it, screaming, and throwing things. Thankfully, it walked away. It didn't run away like I was hoping it would but at least it walked away.

I come back to the tent and see that Mike had left his food all over the ground. He's sitting up now. I guess when I took off after the bear it finally got his attention. I told him we were almost bear food because he didn't go bury his trash like I had asked him too.

He went and buried his garbage but still didn't believe me that there was a bear until the next morning when we walked back to look at the tracks. I have no idea how he slept through all of that. He must have been worn out. Thankfully, I was a light sleeper and already had experience dealing with bears. He may have tried to run if he saw it so it was probably best that he just stayed in his tent.

The next day we were making our way into Hattiesburg when this girl named Jessie sent me a message saying that we could crash at their place for the night. We took her up on the offer and made it there around noon. Jessie had invited one of her friends over, Lauren, so she wouldn't feel weird about having two guys over; but she had been following my page for a while and knew she could trust me.

As soon as we got there they asked if we wanted to go pick up some beer. They said we could get whatever we wanted. So that's what we did. Me and Mike both got a six pack and then they told us to get one more. We laughed and said "okay".

We go back to their house and start drinking, talking, watching movies, and just having a good time. At some point, I hear a knock at the door and I go to answer it. There was a little boy and he asked me if I had any money. I asked him what he needed money for and he said, "My daddy told me to come ask for money for food." I asked him if he had food at his house and he said he did. I asked him why his dad wanted money for food if they had food. And then I noticed he was trying to look around the house.

I knew what he was doing. Someone was sending this little kid out to snoop out things for them to come back and steal. I went outside with the boy and talked to him for a minute. I told him I'd give him $5 if he did twenty pushups. He said "okay" and it took him a while but he finally did them. Then he asked for the $5 and I asked him again, "What do you need money for?" He said, "Because you said if I did twenty pushups I could have five dollars." I told him that was the right answer and that he earned this money, not whoever sent him.

After the little boy leaves, everyone else comes outside to play a drinking game on the porch. At some point, me and Jessie decide to go back inside and watch a movie. Mike and Lauren are still outside talking and drinking.

After the movie goes off me and Jessie go outside to see what Mike and Lauren are up to. Mike had apparently drunk himself out cold. We drug him into the house and let him sleep it off. He'll be feeling that in the morning!

It was still pretty early too. I couldn't believe Mike was already passed out. Me, Jessie, and Lauren went out on the porch to just sit and talk. We left the door open in case Mike started to throw up in his sleep. We sat and talked about all of my travels up this point mostly. Then we went inside to cook some dinner. We watched another movie and then I went to bed.

I was up before everyone else and noticed that Mike was on the couch instead of the floor. I guess he got up at some point. He was too heavy for those girls to lift him. I walked outside to get some fresh air and when I did their security alarm went off and woke everyone up. Whoops!

I didn't know. No one told me about there being any alarm system. It's a good thing Jessie got up so she could turn the alarm off. If it had gone off any longer the police would have arrived and I would have been in bigger trouble than I already was.

We pack up and left Hattiesburg and made our way up to Collins. It was here that we decided to start making our way west. Otherwise, we would end up in Jackson. So, we turned off and made our way for Prentiss. We made it to the Friendship Sanctified Church before dark and put our tents up in the back.

We heard a couple of cars pull up in the gravel driveway and then heard them go into the church. They used the side door that was just to the right of us. We hoped that they wouldn't see us because we were tired, already had everything sat up, and didn't feel like trying to find another place to sleep. Luckily, they left without ever looking around the corner. At least I assume we were lucky. Who knows what could have happened if we were caught but we were satisfied with what we had.

From here we continued we on highway 84. We went through Prentiss and tried to make it to Monticello before dark, but we found Silver Creek and decided to go ahead and call it a day after about eighteen miles. This seemed like a good place to camp. It was between towns and we wouldn't be able to be seen from the road.

We had about three hours of daylight left when we got down there so we went ahead and sat up camp and began gathering fire wood. I didn't think we could have found a better spot for the night but then things started to get a little weird.

As we were gathering up our firewood I told Mike about the time me and Rob had camped under a bridge in California. I told him that this would be the first bridge, at least next to a creek, that I had camped at since then. He was a little freaked out by my story and jokingly said, "If you had told me that before we got down here I would have said just keep walking. I ain't trying to get possessed or have rocks flying all around my head!"

We hung around the fire and played our harmonicas until it was about 10:00 p.m. and then we heard a large splash in the water. Since I had just told him the story we were both kind of freaking out. I turned my headlamp on and wandered back into the woods to see if I could find something that would have made that noise. I didn't see anything and returned back to Mike and our fire.

We began collecting more firewood because we didn't want to be out here in complete darkness in case things started getting too weird. It looked like our fire would burn for a few more hours so we went ahead and went to sleep.

A few hours later something hit the water again and it woke me up. Mike automatically asked, "Jake, did you hear that?" I laughed and told him that I did but it was probably just a branch falling or something. Then we went back to sleep but not for long.

Around 3:00 a.m. we heard things constantly slamming into the water. We both got out of our tents and tried to get the fire back going but we had already burned off all of the dead wood in the area. Everything else was alive and wet from the rain early that morning so we couldn't get the fire going.

Trees were snapping and things kept hitting the water, like something was just throwing boulders into the water as hard as it could. We packed up our things and got out of there! Even as we were leaving we could still hear all of the noises.

Once we got up onto the bridge I shined my light down into the creek and looked around. All of the noises had stopped and I never saw anything. We decided to keep walking until we found a better spot to camp. That was just too much for us. Neither of us have camped under a bridge since then and I know for a fact that I never will again. Maybe it has something to do with me. I don't know. Mike thinks it was Bigfoot, though. It sounds crazy but there really was no reasonable explanation for it.

We ended up walking until we were about five miles from Monticello. We were tired and decided to make our way up to the top of a hill that was right off of the highway. We usually tried to camp in places where we wouldn't be seen but we weren't worried about that right now.

We woke up around 9:00 a.m. so we were able to get a little sleep. It was obvious that where we were at a lot of people must have noticed our tents up on this hill. I was surprised that no cops had been called or stopped by.

We came down from the hill and started walking. We made it about two miles when this lady pulls over and asks if we were the people who were camping up on the hill. We told her that it had been us. Then she handed both of us a bag with breakfast from McDonald's. Awesome!

We make our way into Monticello after eating our breakfast. We went to a gas station to fill up on water and then we began heading north until we came into Georgetown. That put us about twenty-five miles for the day so we were pleased with that.

There was a park with a gazebo just right off of the highway so we walked over to it so we could sit and eat our dinner, and wait for the sun to set. We figured we would just pull out our sleeping bags and sleep right here on the floor. It was still kind of early, though. We probably had two hours of daylight left.

Mike stayed at the park and I walked over to the gas station, which was about a hundred yards away. I just went in to use the restroom and fill up my hydration pack, but I noticed a liquor store was connected to the gas station; so, I thought I'd go in and grab me and Mike a beer.

I made it back over to Mike and told him there was a liquor store over there. He said that I should have picked up a beer. I knew he was going to say that but I had to set him up. This was a dry town. Mike looked at me and said "What? It's a dry town and they have a liquor store?" I told him I walked in there and that's what they told me. They only sold liquor. They didn't sell beer. If you get caught with a beer then you'll end up in jail but you can walk around with liquor all you want. That was a first for us. It's usually the other way around.

While we were sitting there eating our dinner we noticed that this truck had been parked in front of us for a while. Mike smoked occasionally and walked over to ask the man for a cigarette. As he was walking up to the truck the man kept waiving at him to go away and eventually started yelling at him.

He gets out of his truck a few minutes later and walks over to us. He asked Mike what he wanted and he said he was just going to ask him if he had a cigarette. The man gave him a cigarette and called him stupid for approaching his truck like that.

This man was waiting on a drug deal and Mike made it look suspicious by walking up to him. We didn't want any part in that. Whatever happened, happened. That was none of my business or concern. Mike was still learning that it's best to just keep to himself.

We were a little sketched out by what had just happened and decided that we should probably camp in the woods just beside the park. We slept well through the night so I guess it was a good decision. The next day we would be making our way for Vicksburg.

Before we made it to Vicksburg, though, we came through a town called Utica. As we came into town we noticed a gas station and a man noticed us walking by. He asked us if we wanted something to eat so we told him "Yeah! Sure!" He waived for us to come into the store and got us both a bag of chicken liver, rolls, and a drink.

We didn't want to sit around and be in anyone's way so we walked across the street to a church to eat our lunch. It was a small white house that had been turned into a church. We sat on the ground in the shade to eat because, even though it was nearing December (if it wasn't already), it was still really hot. This was the first December that I'd ever spent in shorts and a T-shirt.

While we were eating I called the Holiday Inn and Candlewood Suites hotels in Vicksburg to see if they would be able to offer us a complimentary room. They checked out my blog to make sure that I was legitimate and then gave me a call back. They both said to let them know when we got there and they would give us a room as long as one was available. Awesome!

We made it halfway to Vicksburg when we found a church on a side road. There were a few people outside of their houses nearby and they noticed us walking behind the church but we didn't pay them any mind. We went ahead and put our tents up and got everything ready to turn in for the night.

About thirty minutes later a man pulls up and asks us if we needed help with anything. I didn't really know how to reply to that but I said, "Nah. We're just passing through and decided to camp here for the night."

The man replies, "Oh. Okay. Well, this here is my church. But, I don't guess I mind if ya'll sleepin' here. Is that what ya'll usually do? Just camp behind churches?"

Mike then says, "Well, we wood camp in the woods but

they're dark and scary."

I had to keep myself from laughing because that was the most ridiculous thing I had ever heard. At least from my perspective. I preferred to camp in the woods. We had camped behind several churches, though. However, I was not afraid of the woods or the darkness in the slightest bit.

The pastor turns to look at the woods and then looks back at Mike and says, "Yeah. Yeah, you're right. Those woods sure are dark and scary. Ya'll have a good night now. If ya'll need anything here's my number. Ya'll be safe out there walkin' them roads. People always drinkin' and drivin' around here."

The next morning, we wake up and our tents are finally covered in ice. I was pretty excited about it but Mike didn't seem to be so happy. He wanted to sleep in until it warmed up outside. I made him get up anyways. I was already packed up and ready to go. There were kids standing outside waiting for the school bus so I was starting to freak them out.

We get to walking and finally make it the Holiday Inn in Vicksburg around noon. They were really happy to have us and even got a picture with us. Then me and mike went up to our room and took turns taking showers and doing laundry.

I was just lying in bed, watching the television, when Mike says, "You think Domino's would donate a pizza?" I looked at him like he was crazy and said "What? No. The Hotels are only doing it because they can mark it off on their taxes." Mike decided to call Domino's anyways and I was just sitting there shaking my head the whole time. Then I heard him say "Really? Awesome! Jake, what kind of pizza do you want?"

I was blown away that they had actually said yes. I didn't care what kind of pizza he got. I've eaten pizza out of the trash before and had no idea what was on it. I was pretty excited about it, though. We scored two hotels and now a pizza, too? This was just unreal.

After we finished eating Mike decided to take the pizza box and go fly a sign for spending money. I told him no one would probably give him anything but he looked bad enough so they might. We laughed after I said that and he went out into the street to do his thing.

He comes back about two hours later and said that a police officer made him leave because he was distracting people. I asked him if he had any luck. I was expecting him to say something like five dollars but he ended up with nearly a hundred! That was great! I had a crowd funding site set up so people could help us out, along with a link directly to St Jude Children's Research Hospital as well, but I had been taking almost everything from the crowd funding and sending it to St Jude's. This would help us out a lot!

We get some breakfast here at the Holiday Inn and then walk over Candlewood Suites. It was pretty much the same thing all over again. Minus the pizza and panhandling. Okay, basically all we did here was lie in bed all day and got us a shower in the morning before getting back out on the road; which I was already beginning to miss. It's easy for your mind and body to get out of sync if you don't keep with it. I was ready to get going. Mike was starting to act a little sluggish, though. That's what happens when you take too long of a break.

When we got up to the bridge crossing the Mississippi River we realized there was absolutely no way for us to walk across. We would have to hitch a ride. It didn't take long for a truck to stop and tell us to hop in the back. We didn't even have to say anything. He already knew what we were trying to do.

We finally made it into Delta, Louisiana! That was our three-hundred-mile mark. I always got a rush from every one-hundred-mile mark and each new state. That was part of what kept me going. Mike didn't feel the same way, though. He was beginning to fall apart and had been for about   a   week   now.

9

We had only walked a few miles since we got dropped off at the bridge when he said he wanted to take a break. He had a rash going on downstairs so I understood wanting to take a break for that. When your thighs feel like they're on fire it's time to powder up and keep on moving! That was how I did things anyways. I was still a grunt at heart.

We started walking again and made it about fifty feet when Mike stops and says, "I think I'm done." I told him to sit and think about it until he knows for sure. He made a line in the dirt and said, "If I cross this line I'll keep going." So, we he sat there for a while staring at the line and then he stood up and said, "Yeah, man. I just want to go home. I can't do it anymore."

I had to give it to him. Walking for over a month with forty-five pounds on your back isn't the absolute greatest feeling. I even wondered where I got my motivation most of the time. Of course, for now, my motivation was to raise money for St Jude. That was more of my thing, though. Mike just wanted some adventure and he'd had enough.

There was a bus station right across the bridge so he went back to catch it. I guess that hundred dollars he had made was about to be paying for his way home. And, that's exactly what happened. He headed back to Vicksburg and I continued on by myself. I knew I'd miss his company but now I would be able to start kicking up dust. We had been averaging about twenty miles each day. That was half of what I was used to.

He sent me a message later that night to let me know that he was on the bus heading home. He asked where I was at and I told him that I was camping at a park in Delhi. He asked how far that was and I told him it was about forty miles from where we split. He said that I was crazy (in a good way), gave me props, and wished me good luck.

I had actually made it into Delhi a couple of hours before dark. I could have made it to the next town if I had wanted to but I found a dog to play with and lost track of time. I even carried a bag of dog treats with me while I was walking if that says anything.

The next day, which was December 12, 2015, I ended up getting a motel in Rayville. I didn't want to but there was some severe weather heading this way and I had the opportunity to seek shelter here so I took it. There were a few tornado warnings that night and the following morning, but luckily none of them touched down.

After the storms had passed I continued on and made my way into Start before lunch time. I walked over to a park to have a couple of snacks and noticed a sign that read "TIM MCGRAW WAS RAISED HERE" Not that I cared but I thought that I would share that. I just wanted to eat my beef jerky and be on my way.

I made it into Monroe just before dark and wandered around this gas station picking up change. I probably looked pretty rough doing that but it was more of a hobby than a necessity. It's like metal detecting but you don't have to dig for it. People could think whatever they wanted. I had four dollars in my pocket and that would get me a couple of coffees!

I thought about camping here in Monroe but decided to

go ahead and do some night walking since I was feeling up to it. I was walking through Claiborne just as it was getting dark and these two teenage boys come running up to me. They gave me four dollars and then asked where I was going. I told them what I was doing and they said "Oh! Cool! We just thought you were homeless!"

It wasn't long after that when I noticed that another storm was moving in. I checked my phone and there was a tornado warning heading this way. Awesome. Stuck out in the middle of nowhere in another tornado. I knew I had about fifteen minutes to find a spot to take cover so I began jogging.

I came across a funeral home and decided to make my way underneath the carport. It didn't offer much protection but it was better than being out in the storm. There was a ramp that led up to the back door of the carport (yes, I know what this ramp is for) so I crawled underneath it and pulled my sleeping gear out.

The rain got so heavy, though, that it began to flood and I had to get up and stand up against the wall. The wind was pushing the rain in so it was pretty bad. I stood there for about an hour or so before the worst of it had passed.

At least the wind wasn't blowing the rain in anymore so I was able to sleep on the ramp for a few hours before I had to get up and get out of there. Just before I fell asleep I looked across from where I was lying and there was a sign that read "LIVE LIFE LIKE YOU MEAN IT!" I laughed at that sign because I was trying my best to make the most out of what life had given me. I knew that it could all be worse, though. That was for sure! I was out here trying to help raise money for the children at St Jude. They had it much worse than I did. I knew that.

I probably got about three hours of sleep that night but it didn't stop me from making it into Arcadia. That was about a sixty mile day and half of it I had been marching through the rain. Sixty miles definitely wore me out. Storm or no storm, I would be getting some sleep tonight!

It was still daylight out but I was ready to get some sleep. I was starting to get wobbly. I had pushed myself pretty hard that day. So, I wandered off into the woods not too far from the road but far enough to not be seen. I passed out as soon as I got in my tent.

I made it into Athens in time for lunch. There was a gas station on the northern end of town so I decided to stop by there. I grabbed a beer and a bag of chips. Not the healthiest of lunches but I took vitamins so it was okay!

I took my chips and beer behind the store and had my lunch on this old concrete foundation. It looked like there had been several other people here before me who had done the same thing. I always hated seeing trash. If there isn't a trash can anywhere around at least bury it! What really makes me mad is when there is a trash can nearby and people still choose to litter. Come on now.

I had put down a lot of miles yesterday so I figured I would take it a bit slower today. I just wanted to make it to the next town before dark. As I was making my way through Homer that night I was stopped by a police officer.

I expected him to ask me a ton of questions but he just asked, "Hey! Are you Jake?" I replied, "Yeah. My name is Jake. How's it going?" The officer said, "My wife is following your blog. She said that you were making your way through here and told me to get you a hotel for the night. How does Best Western sound?"

I laughed and told him that sounded awesome! He drove me down to the police station and dropped me off so he could go take care of some things. He told me to go inside and tell them who I was and what I was doing there. He would be back in a few minutes to take me to my hotel room.

When I walked inside everyone was giving me the weirdest look. Like I was about to have some troubling news. I told them that I was just waiting for their officer to come pick me up. I don't guess that really registered for them the way

I intended it to. The lady who was working as the dispatcher walked over and asked me what I was talking about.

I told her that I'm walking across America for St Jude and one of your officers told me to wait here so he could get me a hotel room.

She started laughing and said "Oh! You're that guy! I thought you were some homeless person! Yeah, feel free to just sit and wait. There's water or coffee if you need anything."

I told her that I was "some homeless person". She didn't know how to reply to that. I just love making things awkward sometimes. The officer walked in a few minutes later and we made our way to the hotel.

I had a care package from Jody waiting for me at the post office here in Homer so I went over to pick that up first thing in the morning. There were fourteen packs of tuna, six cans of potted meat, four cans of spaghetti, one can chicken Alfredo, one bag of Corn Nuts, one can of smoked oysters, one bag of dried fruit, two cans of spam, a handful of instant coffee, and two five dollar bills. This was a pretty common care package from Jody!

I was supposed to have a replacement sleeping pad there today, too, but it wouldn't be there until tomorrow. I spent most of the day just sitting around and playing my harmonica. A long boring day but I'd be making up for it pretty soon. I camped behind a church that night.

When I woke up in the morning I noticed that someone was inside so I walked in to ask if they had any coffee. I had the instant coffee but I wanted something to warm me up. The days were hot but the nights were cold.

The man's name was Jerry. He offered me some coffee and told me about someone having cancer in his family. I can't remember who he said it was. I think he said it was his wife but I could be wrong. I'm writing completely out of memory and it's been a while. I do remember his name was Jerry, though! He was super nice and said that I was doing a great thing. When you're wondering if you're on the right track or not it's always nice to hear it from someone else.

After that I go down to the post office and waited for my replacement sleeping pad. It didn't get there until around 2:00 p.m. so I knew it was going to be a short day. Just before I make it out of town a car pulls over.

A woman and three little girls get out and start walking over towards me. They wanted to thank me for what I was doing and gave me a bag of food and a card. Then I got a picture with the girls and they took off. They sure were a happy little bunch!

I tried to eat as much of the food as I could before I continued on. Jody already had my weighed me. I took what was left and strapped the bag to my pack. It made quite a bit of noise which was kind of annoying, but it would help to ward off any bears or boars. That's what I was hoping for anyways.

It wasn't too long of a distance to Haynesville but I was a little skeptical about walking around out here after dark. I had forgotten to charge up my headlamp and my battery packs. So, I was walking in complete darkness after just a few miles. I was about halfway between towns when two cops pull over to see what I'm up to. After I informed them of who I was and what I was doing they went on about their business.

As soon as the police officers were gone I heard something over in the woods. I kept walking and tried to ignore whatever it was but I realized that it was following me. I turned to yell at whatever it was and sure enough it was a boar. Thankfully, it ran off in the other direction. I felt like I could take a boar but it would probably take me in the process. One swift run of their tusk into your leg and you'd bleed out in a matter of seconds.

When I got into Haynesville it was about 9:00 p.m. or so and I went into a gas station to use their restroom and fill up on water. When I was about to leave I ran into two ladies named Stephanie and Taylor. They insisted on letting them buy me something to eat so I did. I think I got a gas station burrito but I don't remember. I remember it was something hot, though. Something that would keep me warm at night.

The next morning, I was making my way into Arkansas when I ran into another army vet named Glen. We talked for a few minutes and he slung me a few bucks. He said he'd been following my blog for a while but wasn't expecting to see me. He said he was sure he knew it was me because of my green bandanna. I was always wearing that thing! I don't really know why. It just became a habit. When I put that thing on then I knew it was time to get to work.

I crossed into Arkansas on December 19, 2015. I put my pack down to get a picture with the state sign and this man pulls over. He said his name was Al and he was a pastor in Magnolia. He asked me who I was and what I was doing out here. When I told him, he decided to give me five dollars but he was still skeptical. He thought I was just some crazy homeless dude. When people gave me money while I was walking, I would take that amount out of my crowd funding site and send that over to St Jude. That's how I kept only what I needed and the cycle going.

It was too long after that and I had made it into Emerson. There wasn't much going on here but I passed by a house where I saw a family outside grilling in their front yard. The man yelled and asked, "Hey, man! You wanna come eat?" So, I walked over and introduced myself to everyone. There was the man who called for me, his wife, a woman about the same as her, a teenage boy and his girlfriend, and a little girl. They were down to earth, funny, southern black folks. I didn't feel like I really fit in with them that well but none of us seemed to care. They were all curious about what I was doing out here and when they found out they wanted me to stick around and talk a little more. I wasn't in a hurry to leave anyways. They were good people and had good food!

I hung out with the Emerson family for about two hours and then got back on the move. It was starting to get dark but I only had twelve more miles until I reached Magnolia so I figured I'd do some more night walking.

When I got into Magnolia I saw this church just off of the side of the road. It was the Mt. Zion Baptist Church. I didn't think about it being Saturday so I slept right in front of the building while I let my things charge up on an outlet.

I didn't use my tent this night. I had just thrown my sleeping pad down on the ground and crawled into my sleeping bag. I must have been sleeping pretty hard because when I woke up I heard footsteps walking along the sidewalk right beside my head. I never heard any car doors or anything.

I heard the church door open and then shut back. I didn't hear anything else for a few seconds so I sat up and popped my head out of my sleeping bag. There was an old black lady walking towards me and she said, "I was wonderin' who that was sleepin' but I just figured I'd let you sleep. We is cookin' in here if ya'll wanna come in an get ya'll somethin' to eat." I replied, "Do you guys have any coffee?" The lady laughed and said "Yeah we have coffee. Come on inside. It's cold out here." So, I got up, got my things together, and went inside.

When I went in I was greeted by a man who I figured was the pastor and the woman who I assume was his wife. They were talking about all sorts of things. It was like they barely even noticed I was there. Not in a bad way but in a way that I didn't seem to be making them feel uncomfortable. Just a real laid-back couple that made me feel at home.

The woman was standing in the kitchen, cooking breakfast and talking away about just whatever. She finally turned and asked me what I was sleeping out there for. I was so shocked that they hadn't asked me that yet. I didn't want to tell them what I was doing at this point. I just told them that I was traveling through.

It was nice to just be treated with care from strangers without them knowing who I was or what I was doing. They just invited me in and made me feel comfortable. They didn't care who I was, the color of my skin, or anything other than seeing to it that I wasn't hungry. She handed me a plate with a couple of donuts and some sausage, and then a cup of coffee.

After I finished my food I thanked them and told them that I had to get back to work. They didn't know what I was talking about when I said "work" but that's how it felt to me. Walking had become my job. A job that I was happy to get up and go to every day! Most of the time anyways.

Just after I left the church I got a message that I had a hotel room reserved at the Hampton Inn here in Magnolia. I also had a package waiting for me when I got there. So, I made my way up to the hotel and checked into my room. I went back downstairs to ask about that package and they handed it to me.

I took the package back up to my room and it was some ointment for the rash I had been complaining about and some new underwear. The underwear that I was wearing had a seam that was just not meant for hiking. I had cuts and burns all over the inside of my thighs. It was pretty bad. Bad enough for someone to go out of their way to send me some Body Glide and spandex underwear specifically designed for hikers. No seams!

I got here pretty early so I didn't know what to do with my time. I went straight to the bathroom and let my body soak in a hot bath. After I got out I felt so much better. I didn't even realize that my body was sore until I noticed how much better I felt.

After I got out of the bath I threw all of my clothes into the bathtub and went to watch some television in my new underwear. Man, those things felt great! As a matter of fact, I still wear those same underwear! Not the same pair, obviously, but the same type and brand. I can't find a pair right now to tell you what they are but I know they're from Adidas.

The next morning, I went down to get my continental breakfast and I was back on the move again. I took some back roads to get back up to the highway. I'm not sure how this lady who was looking for me actually found me but she did. She had her son with her and he wanted to meet me because he had been a patient at St Jude Children's Research Hospital. He had been cancer free for almost two years!

I wish I would have caught their names so I could see how he's doing now. Maybe they will read this book one day and send me a message. Either way, meeting this little guy gave me a lot of motivation. Even to this day when I look at our picture together it gives me motivation. It's unimaginable what these kids, their families, and their doctors have to go through.

I got to stepping after that and found myself ending my night in Stamps. I had planned on doing some night walking but there was some severe weather heading my way so I figured I would just call it a night here.

Ironically, I found myself taking shelter at another funeral home. I don't know what it is about me seeking shelter at a funeral home. It just has a bad vibe to it when you know there are tornadoes popping up all around you.

I laid my sleeping gear out underneath the awning just to the side of the building and waited for the storm to hit. While I was lying there an opossum walked up to me and started checking me out. I told him to get away from me and then he hopped off into someone's back yard.

The storm came and went and luckily it was uneventful. Nothing that I wanted to be out walking in, though. I fell asleep once it had all passed and woke the next morning, packed up, and made my way for Texas.

It was about thirty miles or so to Texarkana but I didn't get there until dark, which meant that I wasn't really in too big of a hurry that day. I guess I was feeling a little down since tomorrow was Christmas Eve and I knew, or at least I thought I knew, that I would be spending the holidays alone.

Looking back at it, I forgot to mention the Thanksgiving I had with Mike. I don't know how I let that slip by me. I don't remember where we were exactly but the day before Thanksgiving we had dinner at some church. The preacher saw us walking along the highway and told us to come eat before everything was gone.

They had most of the food put away or people had taken it home, but we both had us plenty to eat. We got a picture with the preacher and us three together looked like some characters from the movie The Lord of the Rings. If you've ever seen the movie then picture me as Frodo, Mike as Sam, and the preacher as Gandalf. If only had he sent us on this journey would it be perfect!

Anyways, I didn't feel like going into Texarkana after dark so I camped in the woods about a mile out. When I could hear the sounds of the city I knew I was either too close or close enough. I went to sleep and wondered what tomorrow would bring. A new state was the only thing that was for certain.

The next morning, I made it to into the center of Texarkana and claimed my Texas state sign! I was about to be on my way out of there but I had been messaging this girl that I met back in Mississippi. She wanted me to come hang out with her for New Year's so we got me a greyhound ticket for Christmas.

I spent my Christmas Eve night in Texarkana camped behind a church. I had my tent set up within this small fenced in area. There was just enough space me and the air conditioning unit, which ran constantly throughout the night. It wasn't the best Christmas Eve but I knew that I was about to be in some good company.

The next morning, I made my way up to the bus station. I made it a little early so I decided to grab me a cup of coffee from a nearby gas station. I didn't want to be an eye sore so I walked away to sit and drink my coffee away from everyone else in a vacant parking lot.

This old man drives up and tells me to come over to him. So, I get and I walk over to his car. He holds out his hand to give me something so I reached out to take it. It was a plastic coin that had some bible verse on it. We told each other to have a merry Christmas and then he drove off. I didn't really care too much for the coin because I wasn't religious but I went ahead and stuck it in my wallet out of respect. It was Christmas after all.

I finally got on my bus and made my way to Meridian, Mississippi to meet up with Jessica. When I got there, she was busy with her family so I just walked around Meridian for the rest of the day. I ended up going to Walmart and noticed the woods behind it would make an awesome camping spot for the night.

I didn't know what to do with my time so I set up my gear, went back down into Walmart, bought a six pack, and then went back up to my little house on the hill. I still had a few hours of daylight left so I decided to make a video on water purification. Not that it was rocket science or anything, but a lot of people were curious as to how I went about it; and it gave me something to do. Mostly it just gave me something to do.

The next day, Jessica came to pick me up. She had to come to Walmart anyways because she needed some new tires put on her car. We walked around in the store until they were finished and then we went to get a hotel room. While we were in the store we picked up a few board games, a DVD player, and a few movies.

Our first day and night together went really well. I was excited about having some company. I had been wandering around by myself for so long that I don't even know how to explain the feeling. It's almost like being brought back from the dead. When I was walking I was pretty much a zombie. You go a little crazy when you're out there all alone. Even if you don't realize it.

We checked the hotel out again for another night but we didn't want to just sit around all day so she took me to one of her favorite spots to go hiking. We walked around in the woods and I taught her how to set traps. We were having a pretty good time. Nothing too crazy but it was fun.

Once it started to get dark we went back to the hotel and it was basically a repeat of the night before but this time things got a little intimate. That's where I made the mistake. Do not get intimate with someone if you're traveling. That's what I have to tell myself anyways. Everyone's different but I ended up falling in love. I know! I'm so bad about falling in love with people. It's a curse!

I don't think I was in love, though. No. Of course not. But it was a great show of affection that interfered with the communication between my heart and brain. This wasn't a good thing because she didn't feel the same way. It didn't become apparent until about three days later, though. This routine continued so my feelings were growing. We were hoping to spend New Year's together and then I'd get on the bus and head back to Texarkana.

New Year's Eve comes around but Jessica does not. I didn't take that so well because I wasn't used to these emotions. I let my guard down, became comfortable, romantic, and then got kicked to the curb. It was just a good time for things to go bad.

I had the hotel to myself that night and I started to feel suicidal. I don't think it was because of the girl but because of the mix of bad emotions. No one is worth taking your life over. I knew that. That wasn't the problem, though. I was already dealing with bipolar and PTSD. If you throw a match into a fire what do you expect to happen?

I didn't really sit around to put a whole lot of thought into it. Once I had the idea I got out of bed and set up a noose inside of the hotel room closet. I placed it around my neck and just before I let my body drop someone knocked on the door.

I didn't want to get caught so I jumped up, shut the closet door, and went to see who had knocked. When I opened the door to my room there was no one there. I could have sworn that I heard a knock and it didn't take me but a few seconds to get to the door.

I shut the door and turned back to walk for my death trap. I look down and there is a bible sitting right in front of the closet. That was definitely not there when I got up to go check on the knocking so it really got my attention. I'm not a religious man but I've always wondered. It's never too late to be proved wrong. I didn't know what to think about it but it definitely made me stop to consider what I was doing.

I put the bible in a drawer and try to get some sleep. I couldn't sleep, though. I just couldn't stop thinking about hanging myself. It was all I could think about. The whole situation that happened nearly an hour ago wasn't even being processed. I could not think about anything other than just letting go and how peaceful it must be.

I settled on it. It had to be done. There was no other way. Nothing was going to stop me. I was infatuated with the idea of my life being over. I've had suicidal thoughts before but nothing so intense. I wasn't even comparing my options. So, I got out of bed and walked over to the closet. I had all of the lights off, even the television. It was completely dark besides the small amount of light peeking in through the curtains. It was a a straight forward walk, though. This wasn't some elaborate hotel suite with multiple rooms. The closet was just maybe ten feet straight in front me.

When I open the closet door I feel it hit something and whatever it was landed on my foot. I reached down to pick it up and I feel a book. I know what a book feels like. I don't need to be able to see to know that this is a book.

And I knew that it wasn't just any book. I remembered the way that bible felt and this was that bible. I turned the light on and sat on the edge of the bed, holding the bible in one hand and scratching my head with the other.

I'm not religious! This is crazy! Even if there was a God, which at this point I was beginning to feel that there very well may be, why would this God care about someone who doesn't even believe?

I said, "Okay. I've never read the bible in my life. I don't know what you're trying to get at here. I'm going to open this to a random page and by all means feel free to direct me to what it is that you want me to know."

I looked down and read, "FOR I KNOW THE PLANS I HAVE FOR YOU, DECLARES THE LORD, PLANS TO PROSPER YOU AND NOT TO HARM YOU, PLANS TO GIVE YOU HOPE AND A FUTURE."

I sat the bible on the desk in front of me, walked over to the closet, took the noose down, and went to sleep. I woke the next morning feeling confused about the whole ordeal but I didn't feel bad anymore. It was just one of my many experiences that I couldn't explain but I did feel better. I was ready to get back to Texarkana and continue on with my walk.

I arrived back at the Texas state line on January 3rd, 2016, and continued on with my walk. Just outside of Texarkana this young lady pulls up next to me and says, "Hey, Jake! I brought you some lunch." She had been following my blog for a long time but we never talked. She introduced herself like I knew her and I was just standing there wondering how she knew me. That happened a few times. People would say, "Hey, Jake!" and I would feel awkward because I didn't know their name.

She brought me a large drink, fries, chicken nuggets, and a hamburger. I wasn't very hungry but I did eat the chicken nuggets and killed that root beer. I held onto the fries and burger until I ran into someone who looked like they needed it, which wasn't very long.

I passed by a Walmart on the far west side of town and decided to call my doctor to see if he could send in a prescription. I felt like I needed a different antidepressant because the one I was taking was working so well.

I sat around and waited but my prescription never got called in. I'd have to camp around here somewhere and pick my medicine up in the morning. It was only about 5:30 p.m. so I still had plenty of time to find me a good spot to camp.

I walked west from Walmart for about a mile or so and found this old trail. I decided to take it and eventually came across this old abandoned house that had fallen in. Didn't look like anyone had been back here in a while. No trash, foot prints, or tire marks. I felt like this would be a good spot but just for safe measures I decided to go off into the woods quite some ways.

As I was walking through the woods I came across an old grave marker. I found this to be rather odd. There was no trail leading up to it or anything. I took a picture of it but it's hard to make out what it says. I'm sure there is some interesting history to it.

I walked about a hundred yards from the grave marker and found a nice open area in the woods. This would be a perfect place to camp. I didn't have anything else to do besides wait so I went ahead and began collecting firewood. It was finally starting to get cold enough to where I could see my breath so a fire would be nice.

I remember everything was soaking wet, though. I had to strip most of the branches down to nothing to get to the dry pieces. Once your fire really gets going you can throw in some small wet pieces. They will dry out and burst into flames eventually.

While I was back at the store I decided to pick up a couple of beers and a pack of hot dogs. I was having myself an actual camp out it seemed. I had my knives sitting around like they were my company and played them some tunes on my harmonica. Yeah, that is getting a little crazy, huh?

The next morning, I went back to Walmart to pick up my medicine and then I was on my way again. I made it into New Boston just after nightfall and it was really getting cold now. I walked up to a Sonic Restaurant and ordered something hot to eat. I had been trucking along, sweating, and didn't realize how cold it was until I sat down.

I stripped most of my clothing right there in front of everyone. I was just used to it. I gave up worrying about that a long time ago. I was cold and needed to put my base layers on it. Don't like what you see? Don't look! I never had any complaints, though. Ha!

This guy comes out to bring me my food and he sees all of my gear. He asks what I'm doing and I told him that I was walking across America. He said, "Oh! You're that Jake Does America guy! Dude, I read about you a couple of years ago!" He went in to tell his coworkers and they all started looking me up on their phones and giving me a thumbs up.

There was a building just across from Sonic so I decided to camp behind it. It was still rather early so I knew I would be up and out of there before having to worry about anyone. I exercised for about thirty minutes to get myself to nice and warm. Then I jumped into my tent and crawled into my sleeping bag.

The next morning it was snowing and I found my way to the East Texas Trail. It isn't anything worth traveling to. It has a nice ring to it but it was a path of mud that followed along the road. Cars or mud? Pick your poison. I stuck with the trail for as long as I could, though.

I ended my first night on the trail in DeKalb. I still had a lot of energy. The days were just getting shorter. Sometimes I felt like night walking and sometimes I didn't. It just depended on my mood I guess. That night had a lot to do with the weather, though. It had been snowing and raining all day, and my feet were soaked. I could pick up the pace later. Plus, stopping in DeKalb meant that I would have coffee in the morning!

After I get my coffee in DeKalb I go over and get back on the trail. As I was walking along I decided to make a twenty-dollar donation to St Jude from myself. I hadn't been getting a lot of donations on there so I was hoping that would encourage people. I had been walking for forty-nine days so far and that twenty dollars put me just over $1,300.

There was a storm moving in so I went ahead and ended that day in Avery. I had only made it about twelve miles. That was a hard blow but when there was a storm heading for me I took what I could get.

I thought about taking shelter under a dugout at first but then the storm began picking up intensity just before it got there so I began scrambling to find a better place. I wasn't having any luck, though. I ended up pitching my tent next to a church. I camped on the east side of the building so it didn't seem as bad as it actually was.

The next day was January 8th, 2016, which meant it was my twenty-eighth birthday! I wasn't doing anything special for the occasion, though. I just kept walking as usual until I noticed a horse. It appeared as though someone had tied it to a fence with about a two-foot rope. I didn't see anyone so I go over to check on him. I started talking to him but he never moved. I began to wonder if this horse was blind and deaf. I didn't want to spook him but needed to make sure he was okay.

Man! This was a fake horse! Here I had been worrying about this thing and it was fake! I looked around to make sure no one had noticed that I had been fooled. I thought it was pretty funny, actually. I bet they get a lot of people who stop to check on that horse. It looked so real!

Not too long after I had been tricked by that fake horse I had made it into Annona. I don't recall much about it except that it was my seven-hundred-mile mark. Sadly, it was another slow day. I had my reasons to stop in Clarksville. They had a McDonald's here and that meant that I would be able to charge up my electronics and get some laundry done.

My solar panel had been useless for the past two days due to the overcast. If I wasn't documenting the whole thing I would have just kept walking. If I get everything juiced up I could make that power last me a week, though.

With that in mind, I charged up one of my battery packs that night (which took about three hours) and decided to come back in the morning to charge up the other. That meant I'd have a late start and only be able to do a fifteen-mile day ending in Detroit.

I was okay with that once I got there, though. I noticed a store that night which meant I'd be able to grab a cup of coffee in the morning. It was getting down into the teens at night so a hot beverage was a huge boost to get my day started.

I had about twenty miles to Paris, which I was pretty excited about because there was a lady named Delores who said I could swing by to grab lunch. Before I got into Paris, though, a man in a truck stopped me in Blossom. His name was Jerrald and he said he'd seen me walking a few days ago and was wondering what I was up to. After I told him he asked if he could make a donation and wanted to get a picture with me. I thanked him for his support and continued on to Delores's house.

When I got there, she let me eat lunch, take a shower, and do some laundry. While I was waiting for my laundry to get done she even let me take a nap in her son's bedroom. Letting me come over was actually her husband's idea but he was out on a bike ride. He wanted to meet me but I had already left before he had gotten back.

Suno (another solar polar company) wanted to send me out one of their solar panels to test. They had it shipped out for next day delivery so I went ahead and told them to send it to Paris since I was already here. It worked out pretty well, though, because I ended up getting a lot of free gifts from Mobovida, too.

Mobovida sent me a solar powered lamp, two extended

batteries and a glass cover for my phone, a charging port, a charging cable, a waterproof bag, and, most importantly, a good luck card signed by all of their employees!

While I was waiting for those things to arrive I didn't know where to stay, though. I figured I would just walk around and kick cans until it was time to find a place to camp, but I was contacted by Holiday Inn Express. They told me to come over for a complimentary room since I was going to be staying another night in Paris. One of the workers there was following my blog and had the whole thing set up!

Now that I'd had some good rest and relaxation I was ready to hit the road again. I had kind of a late start because I was waiting for all of those things to arrive but I was able to make it twenty miles into Honey Grove before calling it a night. It was dark when I got there so I found a church and tossed my sleeping gear down on the back sidewalk.

I made it into Bonham the next morning and claimed my eight-hundred-mile mark. That's when I ran into one of my followers named Emily. She said she wanted to take me down to Dallas so we could go to a comedy club. I was down for that! It would be nice to get out and have some fun for a change.

She took me out to get some "normal people clothes" (which we returned), ate at the Crab Shack, and then we went to the comedy club. One of her friends was performing and he was actually pretty good. If you care to look him up his name is NickComic. I'm not sure if he's still performing or not, though.

We got a hotel room in Dallas and then the next day she dropped me off back in Bonham so I could continue my walk. I was kind of bored of walking the highways so I decided to take some back roads. I honestly had no idea where I was going and didn't even check my map to see. I just wanted a little change.

It worked out, though. I followed a gravel road for a while

and eventually I came out in Ector. I got back onto a main road here and came into Savoy, put up my tent for the night, and then got an early start. I passed through Bells and then finally made it into Sherman.

I felt like I could go for a couple of beers when I got into Sherman. Obviously, you can't drink beer in public so I had to find a safe place to have a few. I wandered off into the woods when I came across an old couch. No telling how dirty that thing was but it was nice to just plop down and have a cold one, even if it was thirty degrees outside. That's when you go for those seasonal beers!

It started to get late and I didn't want to be walking around drunk so I went ahead and called it a night and camped beside this dirty old couch. These were some rugged times for sure but I was enjoying myself. Looking back at all of it, I think that couch was probably my favorite part of my journey. Okay, not my favorite part but definitely my favorite spot. How often do you just find a couch out in the woods? I don't know. I'm just weird I guess.

The next day I was walking through Sherman when I ran into a lady who had been following my blog. Her name was Christina and she was with her friend Lisa. They picked me up and took me out to eat lunch. While we were eating Christina asked if I'd like to come crash at her family's place for the night so I said sure.

When I got there, it was kind of weird because I looked like a relative and we all got along really well. I got a picture with her, her two sons, and her husband; and I looked like the wild rebellious son. We all had a good laugh about it.

We sat around and listened to music and then they let me play guitar with them. Then it started to get late so they let me get a shower, do some laundry, and then the oldest son slept on the couch and let me sleep in his room. Definitely a nice family!

The next morning Christina took me to have breakfast at her friend's coffee shop back in Savoy. Her name was

Melanie and she was just as nice as the rest of them. A good area just full of good people! Either that or I just got really lucky but they left a good impression.

After we had breakfast I got brought back to Sherman and got another continental room at the Hilton Garden. They let me stay here because I had a couple of tumors that I needed to get removed the next day. One was underneath my tongue and one was back near my tonsil.

Emily came back to take me to get the surgery done and then we got a hotel room so I could recuperate. The surgery wasn't a big deal. The tumors were benign but the shots they gave me made me a little edgy. The pain was tolerable but the adrenaline was something else. The last thing I needed was adrenaline. The hotel was a great idea!

The next day we went off to adventure because she had paid for two nights. We figured we might as well get out and do something. The first thing we did was go down to the Iron Root Republic Distillery and went for a tour. It was pretty cool to see how they did everything and then at the end of the tour they gave us some free samples.

After our tour at the distillery I noticed a large statue of a man's head so I wanted to go see what it was about. The statue was of President Eisenhower. Turns out that he was born here in Denison, Texas and there was even a state park in his name. I was more interested in the state park than a statue so we made our way.

The park had a lot of great hiking trails but I had to do them alone. It was too cold for Emily's liking so she decided to sit in the car. She missed out on some pretty cool spots but from where her car was parked she had a great view of the Red River. You could see Oklahoma just on the other side. I figured I would count that as a state sign even though I wouldn't be going back into Oklahoma. We went back to our hotel room after that and then the next morning I was on my way again. Looked like my next town was going to be Whitesboro. That was only about twenty miles but I had a late start and the days were really short. Once the sun had started to set I put up camp and would be making my way through town in the morning.

I packed up early and got on the move. Not long after I had gone through town, I was stopped by a man, Jack, that I had coffee with back Savoy. I told him about my blog but he didn't seem to be all that interested. I guess he had checked it out, though, because he wanted a picture with me and his dog, Pearl.

I was hoping to get a lot miles down but I was only able to make another twenty, which called for some stealth camping in Lindsay. I was beginning to wonder if I was being lazy, if it was the shortening of days, or if I just didn't care how fast I was going anymore. I'm pretty sure it was the later of the three. I had been out west before. I knew there were going to be those long stretches where speed was necessary. Might as well enjoy myself up until then.

The next day I was walking through Muenster when a man pulls over and asks what I'm doing. After I told him he asked if I would be interested in doing an interview for his radio show. I was expecting to go to a radio station but then he pulled out a tape recorder and began asking me questions.

I was a little worried about how the interview was going to come out because it was on the spot. I had the answers for his questions but I didn't feel like my mind was really prepared for it. He emailed me a copy of it before posting it on his radio station. He edited out the long pauses and awkward sounds of my thought process, so it turned out to   be   okay!

10

I didn't make it much farther after that so it was about another twenty-mile day. I wanted to have a fire and find something to eat so I needed to clock out early in order to get me a good spot. Once I had found what I was looking for, I made it my home for the night and went out for a hunt. I had a few snacks with me but I was craving some meat. Snacks will last you a while but eventually you feel the crash and need some real food.

It only took me about thirty minutes and I had already caught me an opossum. I hadn't killed or even injured him yet, though. I brought him back to my campsite and posted a picture of what was about to be my dinner. Luckily, for the opossum, there was a lady who had been following my blog and she wasn't too far from here. She must have found me from the radio station earlier that day.

I don't know if she felt bad for me or the animal that I was about to eat, but she ended up bringing me a burger, fries, and a milk shake. Honestly, I still wanted to eat the opossum but I let him go to live another day!

The next morning, I continued on and made my way into Saint Jo. I noticed there was a restaurant but I didn't know if I wanted to spend any money on food. I stood there for about ten minutes, asking myself if it was worth it or not. As I was standing there a police officer pulls up and asks me what I'm doing.

I told him that I was currently walking across America for St Jude Children's Research Hospital. I guess he thought I was lying and asked me to put my hands behind my back. He was a scrawny guy and thought that I was trying to resist because my arms were too heavy for him to do anything with them.

He called for backup and just made a huge scene out of nothing. It was really embarrassing, actually. Saint Jo is a small town so I'm pretty sure that everyone saw what was going on and they probably thought there was a bad guy coming through. After about an hour of questioning and digging through my things they finally let me go.

I didn't feel like sticking around here any longer than I had to so I just got back to walking. Before I made my way completely out of town I noticed a store. I decided to stop by and fill up on my water. The cashier told me to be careful walking through here because they have crooked cops, and would likely harass me just because they have nothing to do. I laughed and told him that he was too late. I'd already had trouble with them and he hit the nail on the head when he guessed which cop it was.

The cashier said that same cop gives everyone in town trouble. His wife was working with him and said that she was scared to drive because them. They said if I waited a few minutes they would drive me a few miles up ahead because they would probably come back to mess with me again. They sounded quite sincere when they said it so I took them up on their offer. When they dropped me off they said, "Now all you have to worry about is the mountain lions." We laughed because we all figured I was better off dealing with wild animals than the police of Saint Jo.

After they dropped me off I was able to make it into Nocona just before nightfall. I found me a place to camp right next to a pond and caught me a fish for dinner. It had been a while since I had some fresh food in my belly. I guess dodging that restaurant back in Saint Jo wasn't such a bad idea after all. I'd rather have my dinner right here anyways and in the morning, I'd have coffee waiting for me just right up the road. You can't beat that!

The next morning, I was starting to feel some pain in my big toe. I knew this feeling all too well. I had not lost a toe nail since my military days but I remembered the feeling. Hopefully, it would burst open sooner than later. It wouldn't be long now and I'd be struggling to make five miles in a day. That was a bit of a downer but I'd keep pushing on as hard as I could for as long as I could.

I was somewhere between Henrietta and Ringgold when I noticed this car had stopped about seventy-five yards up ahead of me. At first, I figured it was someone about to try and offer me a ride but I was wondering why they would stop so far away. As I made my way closer I realized that the car was fully loaded with people. There was no way they were going to be offering me a ride. I began to think that I was probably about to come across some trouble but I just kept walking anyways.

I was about thirty yards from the vehicle when a group of teenage girls all jumped out. What a relief that was! It was funny because here I was thinking that I was about to get beat up and mugged, and then these little girls jump out. They heard about me on the radio and wanted to stop and get a picture. I still don't know why they stopped so far away. They had me freaking out over nothing!

I hadn't made it too far after that when another vehicle pulls over. It was a woman and her name was Kim. She was a really pretty woman and a little taller than me. I'll admit that I felt a little intimidated but I wasn't out here trying to look good! She donated twenty dollars and grabbed a quick picture with me. Now I just wanted to make it into Ringgold and call it a night. The sun was going down and I'd be doing some night walking, but I was fine with that. Another town down would make it all worth it in the morning.

It wasn't too late when I made it into Ringgold but it was definitely dark. Just after I crossed the bridge that comes into town there was a woman outside of her house. She was talking on the phone and asked me if I was hungry. I wasn't interested in making some drawn out deal about it. I just wanted to go find a place to put up my tent and call it a night, but then again, I was feeling kind of hungry.

I said "Yeah! Sure! I guess I could go for a quick bite!" The lady then asked her son to go inside and bring me back out a plate of food. That worked out just how I had hoped it would! She pulled the tailgate down on her truck and told me to have a seat.

She was on the phone with her daughter and she was talking to her almost like I wasn't there. I heard the daughter say "Some guy is walking across America and he's eating at our house? Is he cute?" The mother said "Yeah, I guess he looks alright. A little young for me, though!" Finally, the son had brought me my plate which helped to eliminate the awkwardness that I was feeling. I have manners. I can't talk with my mouth full!

I thanked her for the meal and then began my search for a good place to put up my tent. I turned down the road that the post office was supposedly on and planted myself behind an old building. It worked out pretty well for the night but when I woke the next morning there was a man walking around my tent.

I didn't say anything and neither did he. I feel like we were weirded out by one another but I'm not sure who was really at fault here. I guess he wasn't expecting to see a tent across from his house and I definitely wasn't expecting to wake up to some guy trying to figure out who or what I was. They probably don't get a whole lot of travelers coming through here.

I got back on the road and realized that I had thirty-four miles to Wichita Falls. I did some calculations and realized that I was at my 8,400 mile mark since I started back in 2013. That was day sixty-three since I had left Florida for this trek. That gave me the boost to go ahead and speed up my pace.

As I was walking into Wichita Falls, a woman messaged me and asked if I would put up a missing persons post. She said that her husband had left Wichita Falls a few days ago and was walking to her house in Henrietta. I thought that sounded kind of odd because I had just blown through there and I should be making it into Wichita Falls by tonight.

I went ahead and made the post about her husband on my blog. I had thousands of people looking for this guy. Someone eventually found him in Wichita Falls having breakfast at a McDonald's. He never left or cared to get back in contact with his wife. I kind of had a feeling that was going to be the case but it felt good to at least give her some closure. I was also surprised to see so many people saw my post and saw this man within a few hours.

Emily came to meet me in Wichita Falls. I guess she really enjoyed my company but she said this would be the end of the road for her. She liked going for road trips but she knew that the next time she would have a day off I would be long gone.

She hooked us up with a hotel room which was really nice. I needed to get a shower and do some laundry, but I really needed to take a day off because my toe felt like it was ready to pop. We went for a walk around the park but my toe didn't bother me without all of that extra weight. I soaked my foot when we got back to our hotel room but I knew it wouldn't be much longer before the nail busted off.

The next day I passed through Electra, Harrold, and almost made it to Oklaunion. That was my first forty mile day in a while and I was really feeling it. It was hard for me to get any sleep because the pain was so intense. Every pulse felt like someone was hitting my foot with a hammer. I thought about heating up my knife and melting through my toenail to relieve the pressure but it seemed as though I had waited too long. Trying to do anything for it now wouldn't even matter.

The next day was February 1st, 2016 and I was making my way through Oklaunion, Texas. I was having a hard time with my foot but I tried my best to ignore it. I came across this convertible car sitting in someone's front yard that had two manikins of women sitting in the back. That helped get my mind off of my foot for a few minutes.

I had just hit my nine-hundred eighty mile mark in Oklaunion when my toenail finally decided to crack open. I sat down for about an hour to let the throbbing pain subside and then I was limping my way into Vernon. I had a care package waiting for me there and it was only about fifteen miles away. That doesn't sound like a lot but it took me all day to do it. I had to walk on my heel and try my best to not let my toenail hit the top of my boot.

I finally make it into Vernon just as it's getting dark but it got dark faster than it normally did. They sky grew black and the wind began to pick up. I still had five miles to make it into the city limits and there was no way I was going to beat this storm. I walked another mile or so and came across a cemetery.

Around the cemetery were these concrete walls. I knew the winds were supposed to get up to eighty miles per hour and the walls would help to keep me from flying away. The cemetery was the highest point in the area, though. That was just my luck!

I watched the intensity of the storm build over the town as it was making its way straight for me. About ten minutes later the storm was over me and I was right in the middle of it. It was hailing so bad that I'm surprised none of it came through my tent. The lightning was striking all around and I thought I was done for. I'm not sure how I didn't get struck!

The storm finally passed and I was able to get some sleep. The next morning, I waddled down into town to get my care package. When I got to the post office the lady working there, Alyssa, knew who I was and wanted to get a picture with me. It sure did seem as though I was making the United States a much smaller place.

I was about six miles west of Vernon when I needed to take a piss break. I saw this little concrete building and decided to go back behind there to do my business. I can be a little crude but I'm not about pulling my weenie out in front of everyone.

I'm standing there doing my thing and I noticed a dog coming up through the brush. I whistled and called the dog over. It ducked down in the brush and I noticed a long tail go down behind it. Crap! This wasn't a dog! It was a mountain lion!

I put my man hood away and immediately pulled out my bowie knife and bear spray. The cat was just sitting there in the prone position, watching me. I took a deep breath and ran after the cat, screaming for it to get out of there. There wasn't anything else for me to do besides try to intimidate this thing. Luckily, it worked!

After I was certain that the cat had ran off I made my way back to the road. I noticed there was a house about a hundred yards up ahead. When I got there, there was a man and his dog walking around the yard. I didn't want his dog to see the mountain lion and go chasing after it so I told the man what had just happened.

He thanked me for letting him know and he brought his dog into the house. He said they had mountain lions in the area all the time and had lost a few pets because of them. I didn't stick around for any more conversation or whatever. It was just a quick warning and I was on my way out of there.

I made it into Chillicothe that night which was my one thousand mile mark for St Jude Children's Research Hospital. I was halfway across the country and I had only reached five percent of my goal. That was a little depressing but I was trying. Either way I had raised some money. More than what I could have donated without everyone's help. I was starting to lose my motivation but I kept going. Maybe the donations will start picking back up.

I woke up the next morning and it was freezing! I had been dragging along a lot of winter gear but this was the first time that I had to use it. Minus fifty wind chills were coming down from northeastern New Mexico. It was so cold that the only way to stay warm was to keep moving; even after dark. I would sleep in the cold but only for about an hour or so.

When I was thirsty I would have to melt the ice in my canteens. I had to start a small fire to get water every now and then but I tried to use my body heat as much as possible. Since my canisters were made of steel I had to keep them wrapped up and avoid them touching my bare skin. It was quite the struggle just to keep water available but I wasn't sweating either. If I began to sweat I would take a break.

Sadly, that cold front only lasted a few days. It takes a bit more work when everything is freezing up but I put down a lot more miles. It was all about moving. I even ate some of my instant coffee packets and chased them down with ice cold water. It wasn't a pleasant experience but I spent about three days and nights without any stops. Maybe it was just the taste that kept me going. Who knows?

By the time I had made it into Childress the weather was already warming up. I went behind a building so I could remove all of my extra clothing. There were these houses all along the backside of the businesses but I didn't figure I'd bother anyone. The town was really quiet even though it was the middle of the day.

I was packing my clothes into my pack when this elderly lady came out of her back door. I heard her ask if I could see any pecans on my side of the fence. I realized that she was picking pecans so I decided to help her out with that. I spent about an hour picking pecans. I picked until I couldn't find anymore. I told her that was all of them. She laughed, thanked me, and told me to grab a handful for the road.

After I left here I was heading for Memphis (Texas that is). That was only about fifteen miles or so but it ended up taking me all day because the depression was creeping back up on me. I didn't want to let it take over so I got a few hours of sleep and forced myself to get up and hike on into Claude, my 1,140 mile mark!

The next day I was really slow about making it into Amarillo. I think what was making it so hard on me was the fact that I was doing this for a charity but I hadn't even pulled in a dollar in weeks. That was my motivation and it just wasn't working anymore.

I finally made it just outside of Amarillo when these two girls pull over. They asked me if I'd like to ride with them to Tuscon, Arizona. Man, I really wanted to. I was feeling really down. I wasn't bringing in any money for St. Jude and I felt so alone. These weren't just any girls either. They were babes! It was hard for me to tell them no but that's what I did.

I got on my phone and let everyone know what had just happened. People were calling me crazy for turning that ride down. No one was really interested in my walk anymore. I think most of that had to do with Texas. There wasn't really anything for me to post. Between towns it was just flat and boring for days on end. I tried to keep people entertained but there just wasn't anything to entertain them with.

When I got into Amarillo I went to a gas station so I could fill up on my water. As I was walking up to the store I noticed that the girls who had stopped earlier were here. My mind began to race. I felt like everything that I was doing had died down, I was lonely, I was depressed, and these girls looked like a lot of fun. I knew they wouldn't be here for much longer. I'd better think fast!

I walked up to them and asked if they still had room for one more. They were really excited about picking me up for some reason. They were just young and hippie I guess. I could tell it was going to be a great change for me. I wasn't in it for the ride. I just needed some fun in my life and this was the perfect opportunity.

We hung around the gas station and talked for about thirty minutes or so. I was telling them who I was, what I was doing, and how I was feeling. I guess I was looking for some reassurance that I was doing the right thing because I felt kind of guilty for abandoning my walk. I wasn't hard to convince, though. The way things had been dwindling down left me in a vulnerable state of mind. I jumped into the back of their van and we were heading for Arizona!

We drove for a couple of hours and spotted a place on the map that looked like it would be fun to visit, and maybe even camp for the night. It was a large canyon type of area and there were no other people around for miles. One of the two girls kind of wandered off on her own while me and the other sat and enjoyed the view. This girl's name was Kaylee and she was gorgeous. It didn't take long for us to warm up to one another and it was pretty obvious that, well, basically she had claimed rights to me. Not that we were dating but for the time being we would be a little closer than most people. Ha!

Her friend, Sara, wandered her way back to us just before dark. We decided to go ahead and camp here for the night so I went to their van and pulled out my pack. I had a two-person tent but we would all be able to fit in it without any problems.

After our sleeping arrangements were set we decided to make a fire. There wasn't a whole lot to burn around here but we were able to find enough to last us a couple of hours. Just something to kill the time and bond over really.

That night ended up getting a little wild. I had two chicks in my tent and they both wanted me. Good thing they weren't arguing about it. This was a lot better than walking through Texas feeling miserable. A whole lot better! I'm not going to go into details but feel free to use your imagination if you want!

The next day we made our way into Tucson, Arizona where we parted ways. They were going to some rock festival thing or something like that and then they were heading back home. I think they said they were from Mississippi but it's been a while. They were from somewhere in that direction. They offered to let me ride back with them but I wasn't done yet. Maybe my blog had died down but I still wanted to make it across America again. One way or another.

One of my followers, Kevin, was driving a truck from Tucson to Phoenix and offered me a ride up. I took him up on that because that's where Jody lived. We had become pretty good friends over the years and I was excited to be in his area.

It was February 13, 2016 when I got to Phoenix. Kevin dropped me off at a truck stop and then Jody came by to pick me up. He and his wife, Lisa, were on their way to a family reunion. I didn't know until I was already in their vehicle or I would have told them to wait until after. Jody wanted to show me off to his family, though, so I guess it all worked out. His family were all really nice, there was a lot of food, and they even made me get in the family picture!

After the family reunion, we went back to their house for a few hours. They let me get a shower and do some laundry, and then we went out to see what we could get into. We ended up searching for a karaoke bar and finally found one. I can't remember which one it was but I don't guess that really matters. There are tons of them in Phoenix.

The karaoke was my idea but I had never done karaoke before. I had to get a few drinks in my system before I felt loose enough to sing in front of all these strangers. I had played in bands before but just standing there by yourself and singing in front of everyone is a little intimidating. Until Jody offered to get me a few shots of whiskey anyways. I didn't care much after that.

I was so buzzed that I couldn't read the screen but I knew most of the words. I probably sounded better in my head than I actually did but I had fun with it. I kept trying to sing as many songs as I could but they eventually cut me off. Must have been pretty bad!

At some point, I asked Jody if he wanted to arm wrestle. It was funny because he was about three times my size. We were going at it for about ten minutes or so. We were both shaking and sweating but neither of us were showing any sign of moving. It was all about who's muscles would give out first and we had quite the crowd around us.

I ended up slamming Jody down and it blew everyone's mind. It even blew my mind. This guy was like a giant compared to me. I never expected that! When I challenged him to an arm wrestling match I did it kind of jokingly. In all fairness, though, I had been doing hundreds of pushups every day for the past couple of years.

I've seen videos of people breaking bones while arm wrestling. I'm just glad it didn't come to that because we were both putting in all we had. Both of our arms were sore for about a week after that. I do not condone arm wrestling. I haven't arm wrestled since. I'm just going to hang onto my title unless he ever wants a rematch! We went back to their house after that and I crashed on the couch.

The next day his daughter dropped off her kids. I met Jody and Lisa's grandchildren back in Flagstaff about a year ago. They still remembered me as "that backpacking Jake". They weren't as shy as they had been a year ago. Jody must have talked about me so much that I had become a normal part of their lives. We went out to eat lunch at the Black Bear Diner and then we went exploring the hills around Salt River and Theodore Lake.

We went back to their house after that. Me and Jody ended up watching some movies in the living room until we passed out. The next morning, I had received a message from Kaylee saying they were heading over to San Diego and that I could join them if I was still in the area. Jody and his family offered me a ride to Gila Bend, which isn't too far southwest of Phoenix.

We met up at a McDonald's right off of the interstate and got a group picture together. I thanked Jody and Lisa for the ride and their hospitality for the past few days. I jumped in the driver's seat of the girl's van because they were sleepy and we high tailed it for San Diego.

We made it just outside of San Diego before we were ready to crash. It was about 11:00 p.m. when we got to El Cajon and I had driver's fatigue. The sun had been blinding me all day and I had a pretty bad headache from that. I couldn't drive that stretch every day. I feel sorry for the people who have to. It was pretty cool driving through the desert but the sun was just brutal on my eyes.

We ended up camping behind a Walmart but we weren't the only ones with the same idea. We thought we were alone but after lying there for about an hour we heard some people fighting in the distance. We tried to ignore it but then these people came walking down from the hills and walked up to us. We were camping next to a trail so it wasn't like they were deliberately walking towards us, though.

It was a man and a woman. They said there was another couple up there fighting and that we should be careful because it looked like they were on drugs. I wasn't surprised. We were all too tired to be bothered by it unless they came down closer to us. If they did ever come down none of us noticed because we passed out and didn't wake up until the next morning.

We headed back down to the parking lot, got back into the van, and made our way into San Diego. We went straight to Dog Beach and hung out there until it got dark. Kaylee and Sara made some friends in Tucson. They lived in San Diego and invited them over to crash for the night. I wasn't invited but I didn't mind. I decided to sleep on the beach.

Sleeping on the beach turned out to be a bad idea. I thought I was hidden but someone must have seen me. I was packing up just after sunrise whenever two police officers approached me. There was no way they could have seen me. Someone must have called them and reported that I was sleeping on the beach.

They ended up handcuffing and going through all my things. They wrote me a ticket for sleeping on the beach and let me go. I wasn't in my tent or anything. I should have lied and said that I had just came down a few minutes ago to do some yoga or something. Too late for that, though. I was already sick of San Diego so I made my way to the bus station so I could get the heck out of there.

I was running low on cash so I decided to sell my tent so that I could pay for the ticket that I got for sleeping on the beach. That was kind of like selling my home but I had a tarp for emergencies. The tarp would be fine for the time being.

After I sold my tent and paid for my ticket I made my way up to Long Beach. I'm not exactly why I chose to go to Long Beach but it turned out to be a promising idea. Unbeknown to me, one of my followers, Andrea, lived here and invited me over for a couple of nights.

We didn't do a whole lot but that was fine with me. It was nice to just sit around and be lazy for a couple of days. Maybe it was just me. The depression was creeping back up on me but I was trying my best to hide it. I was always smiling and making it appear that I was having a blast but I was falling apart on the inside.

I left Long Beach after a few days and made my way up to Redondo Beach. It was dark whenever I got there so I went down to the beach and tried to sleep behind a bench that was on one of the sidewalks. People kept coming and going all throughout the night, though.

So, I made my way back up into town and climbed up on top of some building. There was nowhere to hide but surely no one would bother me if I was sleeping up on a roof. A group of people saw me coming down in the morning but it was too late for anyone to question what I was doing.

I was making my way up to Venice when I noticed there was a group of older people partying outside of a beach house. There was two men and two women. One of the men told me to come over and have a beer with them. I thought, "Yeah, I guess I could go for a beer." So, I went up and introduced myself to them. It became apparent that these people were filthy rich and here I was. I don't judge people by what they have but it just isn't normal for millionaires to talk to hiker trash.

We ended up going out on their yacht and putting down a lot of drinks. I don't really remember much after that. I may have been drugged for all I know. I woke up the next morning feeling really confused and my wallet was missing. I had never been on a yacht before and I had some troubles getting the door open but I finally got it. My wallet was sitting up on top and we were tied down at the port. I'm not sure where everyone went or how I ended up there but I gathered my things and got back onto the move.

I made it into Venice before dark and I got picked up by a girl, Cynthia. We went to high school together and she had moved out here several years ago. It was a small world and I just kept making it smaller! We went out to eat and then headed back to her house. I stayed the night with her and her kids. It was nice to have a safe place to sleep and do a little catching up with an old friend.

The next morning, I walked outside and I noticed that she lived next to Mt. San Antonio. She was at work and her kids were at school so I sent her a text letting her know that I was heading up to the mountain and thanked her for letting me crash at her place.

I was looking online to see what kind of trails I could find that led up to the peak when I read that the mountain was currently closed to hikers due to many recent accidents. Normally, I would ignore mountain closures, but they were handing out fines and jail time to anyone caught up there. I decided that I'd just make my way back to the beach and keep heading north.

I made my way through all the wild cities and rich neighborhoods and found myself in the Topanga State Park. It felt great to get away from all the people. My anxiety had been escalating over the past few days and this was just what I needed to help calm my nerves.

After spending a night out in the forest, I was ready to put some more miles down. I climbed to the highest point that I could find and I was overlooking Malibu. I found a trail up here that would take me all the way into Oxnard. I wasn't in any hurry, though. It took me two days to reach Oxnard but it was nice walking along the mountains with a constant view of the ocean.

After I reached Oxnard I tried to get down to the beach but there was no way. All access points were flooded so I ended up sleeping in a dirt field. The next morning, I made my way back into town so I could take a train up to Santa Barbara.

When I got to Santa Barbara I made my way to the beach pier and noticed a man making a sand sculpture. The sculpture was of two military men. One of them was giving aid to the other who appeared to have his legs blown off.

I asked the man how long it had taken him to make this because there was such detail. He said that he comes out every morning and starts from scratch. Most of the time when he comes back the next day there's nothing left anyways. People usually come through after dark and kick his work over.

He had a bucket leaning over next to the pier and he was asking money from people who were taking pictures. I took a picture and threw in a couple of bucks but most people just took a picture and kept walking. This was obviously how he made a living and the people who weren't supporting him didn't seem to give a shit. Don't want to support the artist? Don't take a picture! People can be so rude. If I had the money I would sit there all day and pay for the people who disrespected him. I saw that kind of mess everywhere I went, though.

I went up to the boardwalk so I could find a place to charge my phone. I noticed an outlet on the outside of a building and plugged into it. After about five minutes of sitting there a man begins screaming at me for stealing electricity. I asked him if he was the manager of this building because I would give him fifteen cents to charge my phone. Instead of answering me he called the cops.

There was a pedestrian standing at the crosswalk just in front of me and he witnessed the whole thing. I got my backpack and began to walk across the street with him when the light turned. He looked over at me and said, "You aren't from around here, are you?"

I headed back down to the beach and hung out near the water for a few hours. I got bored of that so I went up to this little park area where I ran into a man who had been homeless around here for the past twenty years. The only reason I know is because I approached him out of curiosity.

He had a trailer on the back of his bike but the trailer was huge! He had built it himself so that he could live in it. He purposefully designed it so that he would be within all legal codes. He said that he must make changes to it every now and then to keep up with the law. It was made entirely out of scrap parts that he had picked up over the years. I was really impressed!

I was starting to get hungry so I began walking around the streets, looking in garbage cans to see if I could find anything worth salvaging. I ended up finding half a bag of cereal. It was full of ants too! Sounds kind of gross but the ants were an excellent addition for protein. The cereal itself was mostly carbohydrates and sugar. It was a good find! A few people saw me grab the cereal out of the trash and I could hear them talking about it and making sounds like they were disgusted but I was really pleased with it.

I took my bag of cereal and walked back to where I had met the homeless man with the large bike trailer. I wasn't looking for him but I did notice that he was gone. I was just scoping the area out for a place to sleep tonight.

The park seemed to be rather open so I left and walked down the street to a gas station. I needed to fill up my water and use the restroom, and maybe I would spot a place to sleep along the way. I noticed there was a fence with several trees beside it. I got my water and made my way back to this location. It appeared to be well-hidden so I made my way into the trees.

There was already someone in there. It was a homeless man but he said I wasn't bothering him, and I could stay if I wanted. I decided to sit with him because everywhere else seemed to be really cluttered, busy, and occupied.

We were sitting there talking for about an hour when we heard someone walking up to us. The trees separated and another man came crashing through. I immediately recognized this man's face. It was the pedestrian that I had crossed paths with earlier.

He looked at me and said, "Hey! You're that guy that was charging his phone this morning! I got arrested because of you!" I looked at him with a confused look on my face. He said, "Yeah! That guy that called the cops told them that I was with you so the cops found me and took me to the station for interfering with their investigation. They finally let me go but I had to sit in jail all day."

The odds of that happening and then meeting up with this guy in a random patch of trees was just too weird. I apologized for what had happened but he didn't seem to be too bothered by the incident. He was kind of laughing it off as them just being ridiculous and having to arrest someone because there was a call.

Anyways, this little spot was getting crowded so I made my way out of there and went back to walk along the beach. Darkness came and before long it was maybe 3:00 a.m. I wasn't tired so I figured I would just walk around until morning, get a cup of coffee, and keep heading north.

I went out onto a smaller pier that was up some ways from the previous larger pier that I had been on. It was more like a sidewalk that went out into the ocean and looped itself back to the beach. The water began hitting the sides and splashing up on me so I got out of there before I ended falling in. I was completely soaked, though.

I checked my wallet to make sure nothing important had been ruined. Sure enough, my military discharge paper was destroyed. It had been hanging on for its life for several years. There was no way it could have survived a splash of water. I never needed it anyways. I just always carried it in case something came up. When I tried to pull it out of my wallet it literally fell apart. There was no saving it so I ripped it apart and wadded it up the best that I could before tossing it into the trash. I'll just have to request a new one later. No big deal.

As I was leaving the pier I was approached by two men and a woman. They had fishing poles with them so I assumed they were just going to walk by me and head up the pier. When they get close one of the men shoves me and the weight of my pack makes me fall back. I wasn't expecting them to do that so I was light on my feet.

My adrenaline automatically kicked in and I jumped up. They started screaming at me to get out of there because this was their town and they were sick of seeing homeless people every time they wanted to go fishing. I tried explaining to them that I was just passing through but they couldn't hear me because they wouldn't stop yelling.

The guy shoved me again because I hadn't left and I

was really starting to get ticked off. It was like something snapped inside of me and I just froze. I was watching and waiting for one of them to make any sudden movements. I could see them yelling but everything was silent.

I'm not sure what was said but one of the guys swung at my face and I dodged it. He followed through with his swing which gave me a perfect opportunity at a quick jab to his jaw and it knocked him out. The other guy tried to swing at me and I did the same thing to him. So now both of these guys are knocked out in front of me and this woman is screaming at me to get out of there before she calls the cops.

I left after that but I wished I would have called the cops. Even though I knocked those two guys out it was still self-defense. The cops probably wouldn't believe my story, though. Who do you think the cops are going to stick by? Residents or some random traveler? I went down the bus station and got a ticket for Santa Cruz.

I chose Santa Cruz because the ticket was cheap and I knew the area. I knew I probably wouldn't have any problems from here on up to at least San Francisco. San Francisco had been a goal of mine for a few months now. I really just wanted to make it to the Golden Gate Bridge. I felt like I was in the clear now.

I walked from Santa Cruz up to Half Moon Bay which took me about three days or so. I took a lot of trails this time instead of following the highway and it was actually quite pleasant. The trails in this area reminded me of Ireland. It didn't feel like I was in California at all.

I remembered all of the people that I had met in Half Moon Bay and was hoping that I could find them and spend some time with them. I was in a really bad state of mind and really needed someone to talk to. I wasn't wanting to talk about what I was going through or anything but just wanted to have some normal, laid back conversation. Maybe share a few laughs or whatever. Just something to get me feeling a bit more positive.

Unfortunately, that wasn't the case.

Both of the women that I had made friends with were dating someone at the time so they both ignored me. I guess I can understand that. They didn't want their boyfriends to get mad or jealous. So, then I went out to search for Bill.

I ran into a guy that I saw hanging around with Bill a few times before I left the last time and I asked if he knew where Bill was. He seemed to not know who I was talking about so I showed him a picture that was on my phone. He looked at the picture for a few seconds and said, "Oh, yeah! Bill! He passed away."

Man, that was a low blow. I didn't have anyone here to turn to. I just wanted someone to talk to but I wasn't in the mood to make any new friends. I was low on cash and wanted something to occupy my mind so I decided to hang around for a few days. I would make and sell several bows before heading out.

I was selling my bows for fifty dollars and I sold about eight of them. I got me a new pair of clothes, a haircut, and went out to eat at some restaurant down town. I just wanted to feel kind of normal and fit in with everyone for one day before making my way up to San Francisco.

It was dark whenever I got to the restaurant and I decided to go to their outdoor patio to eat my dinner. They had these umbrellas out there but they weren't in the base that holds them. I ended up tripping over one of the tubes and fell on it. The steel pipe almost punctured through my gut. How it didn't go right through me was a complete mystery.

I went to the hospital the next day to see if I had any internal damage. I don't know why I even bothered to go to the hospital but I did. It wasn't like I really cared. If I cared at the time I would have filed a lawsuit for the restaurant having these poles sticking up from their patio, and no lights where people can see where they're at.

The hospital took some x-rays and said that I was good

to go. I had some small tears in my muscle and a huge bruise but it would heal on its own over a few weeks. I was just asked to take it easy for a while.

I left the hospital and made my way for San Francisco. It was around 3:00 in the afternoon when I left the hospital and I had about twenty-five miles to go. I wouldn't make it to San Francisco that day but that's exactly what I wanted. I planned on reaching the Golden Gate Bridge that night so the timing worked out perfectly.

I finally reached San Francisco and the hills were wearing me out. I was so tired that I was swaying all over the place. I decided to call it a night and began looking for a place to sleep. I was pretty close to the Golden Gate Bridge so at least I was satisfied with that. I posted an ad on Craigslist that I was looking to purchase a gun. I didn't specify why but I was planning on jumping off of the Golden Gate Bridge, as I had been for several months, but I wanted a backup plan. I had a bottle of sleeping pills and anxiety medication.

I planned on taking them once I got up to the bridge. I wanted to position myself so that when I finally passed out I would just fall over and land in the water. I wanted to have a gun in case someone tried to interfere with what I was doing. Not that I would turn the gun on them but I would be able to turn it on myself. That was the whole point of making it there after dark.

Well, someone finally responded to my ad and we made plans for me to pick the gun up. Little did I know that it was actually a cop and I had told them about my plans. They made it sound like they were just a curious civilian and didn't care what I did with the gun. Eventually, they asked me where I was at. That immediately caught my attention. I knew that I had been talking to a police officer this whole time and they were trying to locate me.

I hid my blog from the public, turned my phone off, and went to sleep on a tennis court. I woke up the next morning to the sound of people playing tennis. It was probably 5:00 a.m. and raining. I looked over at them like they were crazy but here I was lying in my sleeping bag in the freezing rain, getting ready to go jump off of a bridge. Maybe today would be the day that something changed my mind, though. I figured I owed myself that much so I went back into town to grab a bite to eat.

After I ate my breakfast I turned my phone back on, turned my blog back to public, and then I noticed I had a lot of emails. There were so many people looking for me. None of them knew anything other than the fact that I was a cross country hiker and a veteran. Funny enough, there was another cross-country hiker coming into San Francisco that day and he was also a veteran! What were the chances in that?

I only found this out because one of the emails asked me if my name was so-and-so. I found this to be very odd and used that name in an internet search followed by "walks across America". At the current time, there were only two people walking across America and we were both in the San Francisco area. I looked him up and found out where he was exactly.

He was supposed to be reaching the beach not far from where I was at in just a few hours. I found out what street he was on and went to go meet up with him. I wanted to congratulate him on completing his trek but I also wanted to see if he had received any weird messages from the blog he was running. He wouldn't have any idea who I was so I could have come up with any explanation for asking.

I met up with him around 2:00 p.m. or so and he turned out to be a self-absorbed jerk. I didn't even care to try and talk to this guy about what was going on. He was just tugging along his little cart and had a lot of cameras following him. They had the street blocked off for him and everything.

I was still curious to see if he would be approached by any police officers in regard to a possible suicide case so I walked with him from the sidewalk. We ended up getting down to the beach and there was a huge celebration for him. There were cops all around too but none of them seemed to be questioning him. They were just keeping people and traffic back. I assumed that they must have given up on trying to locate who was asking for a gun.

It was about 4:00 p.m. when I made my way up to the Golden Gate Bridge. I stood there and looked at it from a distance and finally decided that I would try to walk across it. If I got half way across and decided to jump then that's just how it was going to go. I was set on trying to make it without any problems, though. I wanted to defeat my suicidal thoughts.

I was just making my way to the bridge when I was bombarded by police officers. They had found my blog and had been waiting on me since last night. I tried telling them that I just wanted to make it across the bridge but they insisted that I be taken to the VA.

I had never been to the VA before this so I didn't have a VA card. My military discharge paper was ruined about two weeks ago back in Santa Cruz. They couldn't find me using my social security number. I had to sit there and answer a lot of questions about my military experience just for them to let me in. I couldn't believe they had no better way of pulling up my records.

I was in the hospital for about a week before they let me leave. It was actually a pretty nice experience because I was around other veterans and they were all going through some tough times. I didn't feel so alone anymore. I wouldn't have checked myself in. I'm just too stubborn to do something like that. There's no telling what would have happened if I didn't get caught so I have to thank the police of San Francisco for picking me up.

After I got released from the hospital I noticed that they had confiscated my bowie knife, pocket knife, bear spray, machete, paracord, flint, and lighter. I was told upon entry that all of my items would be returned to me but they said, "We don't know where those items were taken."

I was a little ticked off about that but there was nothing I could do about it. I tried calling the police stations all around San Francisco but I had no luck. I don't guess it really mattered, though. I just hoped that I wouldn't need any of those things.

I made my way back up to the Golden Gate Bridge and one of the cops that I saw the week before asked if I wanted a ride across the bridge. I told him that I wanted to walk across if that was okay with him. He asked if I was going to jump. I told him that I wasn't so he told me to go ahead.

I kept stopping because my knees had hardly any cartilage left in them. I must have made the police nervous because they sent a lady on a bike out to check on me. I told her that I wasn't going to jump. I was just having trouble with my knees.

Seriously, the pain was excoriating. I made it across the bridge and realized that I was done. I couldn't walk anymore. I got some x-rays on my knees while I was in the VA and they said I may end up having to get double knee replacement surgery. I don't know how I had made it as far as I had but I was done.

I slowly made my way to a Western Union and had my mom transfer my money into my bank account. I was going to get a bus from San Francisco, California to Fort Walton Beach, Florida. I didn't feel like a failure like I thought I would. I walked until I physically couldn't anymore.

I met up with my friend, Christy, and she brought me back to her place back in Woodland. I stayed with her for about a week while I was waiting for my bus out of San Francisco. She had recently moved into a new house so I helped out with some landscaping, painting, and getting the floor ready for new tiles. It was a lot different than the last time I had visited. My body had grown old and I wasn't the party animal that I was the last couple of times we had met.

When the time had come, Christy gave me a ride to the bus station. We both knew that I had changed. I was a completely different person. For so long I had felt confused but now I could see everything for what it was. I was sick. The past few years had been me coping with my post-traumatic stress and bipolar disorders.

I suppose that's part of it, though. Some people will search for coping mechanisms for the rest of their lives and never find what they're looking for. Luckily, I have found a healthy means of doing so. Most people turn to drugs or alcohol and all I wanted to do was help raise money for charities. I fed off of it. I guess in that sense it can also be unhealthy, though. I would put myself in risky situations, yes, but the main problem would come from being let down.

With my post-traumatic stress disorder, I feel a lot of guilt. Every time I give or someone gives on my behalf, I receive a personal sense of forgiveness. Once I caught onto that I became addicted to it. That also tied into me having bipolar disorder.

When I was manic I would have a ton of energy that I could use to gain more donations and the more donations that I got the more manic I would become. Both of my disorders were feeding off of one another.

If I wasn't getting donations for these charities then I began to feel like a failure. I would spiral into a depression which would lead to a mixed episode where I was basically lashing out with ideas, trying to figure a way out. This would lead to some very impulsive actions. Now, that I understand all of this, I know that I need to get some rest because there is still much work to be done.

73815992R00149

Made in the USA
Columbia, SC
18 July 2017